OETKER

GERMAN HOME BAKING

ORIGINAL GERMAN COOKIES AND PASTRIES

COMPILED IN THE TESTING KITCHEN

OF AUGUST OETKER BIELEFELD

PUBLISHER:

CERES-VERLAG RUDOLF-AUGUST OETKER KG BIELEFELD

Printed in Germany by Druckerei E. Gundlach KG, Bielefeld

Ownership, copyright and all other rights reserved in all countries
by Ceres-Verlag Rudolf-August Oetker KG, Bielefeld

Third edition

ISBN 3-7670-0037-7

This new edition and translation of Dr. Oetker's baking book "German Home baking" offers a comprehensive variety of suggestions for home baking and aims at encouraging housewives to discover the pleasure which comes from baking one's own cakes and the excitement of trying out new recipes.
We hope that this book of traditional German cake recipes, all tested carefully in the Oetker model kitchen, will help housewives everywhere to ring the changes and ensure that the whole family can share in the pride and pleasure of home-baked cakes.

AUGUST OETKER BIELEFELD

TABLE OF CONTENTS

GENERAL RULES FOR BAKING 7

CAKES MADE BY THE CREAMING METHOD 10

CAKES MADE BY THE KNEADING METHOD 34

THE "FIVE MINUTES" PASTRY 70

SPONGE CAKES 82

CHOUX PASTRY 132

BAKING OR FRYING IN DEEP FAT ... 140

CAKE MAKING AT CHRISTMAS 142

CAKE MAKING WITH YEAST 161

ALPHABETICAL INDEX 169

GENERAL RULES FOR BAKING

The right Tools
A pair of scales should be available for weighing the ingredients or at the least, a measuring beaker. A jug for liquid measurement is also a necessity; success can only be assured by accurate measuring of the given quantities.
The mixing bowl should be of china, stone or earthenware with smooth sides and rounded corners. Enamel is not advisable as it could chip and an aluminium bowl may discolour the cake mixture. Place the bowl on a wet cloth or in a special holder before beginning to mix to ensure a firm base.
The many Dr. Oetker baking utensils now available have been well tested and are to be recommended. Cream butter and sugar with a wooden spoon (preferably with a hole) and prepare sponge mixture with a really efficient whisk. A good sieve is indispensable for sieving flour or icing sugar. A spatula or plastic scraper is very practical for removing the last remnants of cake mixture from the bowl and for smoothing it evenly over the baking sheet (dip in milk or water to prevent mixture sticking to scraper). Recipes in this book for cakes in round tins contain enough mixture for a tin of 26 cm ($10^1/_2$ in.) diameter.
Always clean baking tins, sheets and moulds thoroughly after use, washing and drying them carefully.

Good quality ingredients
Do not risk spoiling the cake by using inferior ingredients. Flour should be dry and on no account should it be lumpy or damp. Oetker Baking Powder should be bought fresh in small quantities when needed. If a small amount is to be stored, or an opened packet, keep in a cool dry place and away from strong smelling goods (e.g. spices). It is best stored in a tin with a tightly fitting lid. Use castor sugar if at all possible as it is absorbed better and more quickly. Under some circumstances using very coarse-grained sugar can ruin a cake. Eggs should be as fresh as possible – break each egg into a cup first to check its freshness.
Whisked sour milk or buttermilk may be substituted for fresh milk. Any cottage cheese used in a recipe should be fresh, sweet and dry.

Careful preparation of cake mixture
In preparing the cake mixture always be guided by the general rules for that particular mixture which are given as an introduction to the recipes.

Baking the cake
To obtain a perfect cake a cook must not only follow the mixing instructions carefully; she must also know her own oven.

a) Gas and Electric ovens without a Thermostat
The following chart of oven temperatures has been tested and found successful.

Oven description	Electricity		Gas
	Temperatures in C	Temperatures in F	Standard Regulo Mark
Slow Meringues and macaroons.	130°–160°	265°–320°	2 or under
Moderately hot Cakes made by the creaming method in large or medium-sized tins. Medium-sized tins with creamed mixtures and fruit. Sponge mixtures (flans, tarts, sponge sandwiches).	170°–200°	340°–390°	2–6
Hot Flat cakes (oblong tin or baking sheet), cakes in patty tins and biscuits.	200°–225°	390°–440°	6–8

Gas and electric ovens heat up quickly and so a number of cake types may be placed in a cold oven, for instance, cakes in deep tins like Fruit Cake or King's Cake. Cakes on a baking sheet on the other hand require a preheated oven so that they retain their shape, e.g. biscuits, Stollen. A different make of oven could cause the baking time to vary a little; we recommend looking into the oven more often towards the end of baking time. Take care when putting the cake into the oven that it is standing horizontally and that the mixture is evenly distributed in the tin. Place all tins or moulds on the grid, not on a baking sheet or on the bottom of the oven; this latter will cause the cake to become too brown underneath. It is also important that the cake should be baked at the right height in the oven, according to the depth of mixture in the tin. A good rule is- the deeper the tin, the further down in the oven, e.g. Fruit Cake should be placed on the grid at the lowest shelf setting. Shallower mixtures in round cake tins or ring forms should be placed on the grid at the lowest shelf setting if there are three in the oven and at the third if there are four. Stollen should be placed in the middle of the oven or, if there are four settings, at the second from the bottom. Baking sheets with biscuits or small cakes should be placed at the highest shelf setting in gas ovens. In electric ovens with three shelf settings place the baking sheet in the middle, in ovens with four settings at the second from the top.

Before removing larger cakes from the oven test by piercing the middle with a thin wooden stick. If this comes away clean with no damp crumbs sticking to it the cake is done.

b) Gas and electric ovens with thermostat

Most modern ovens are thermostatically controlled, that is to say the oven is heated to a certain temperature and automatically maintains that temperature. Electric ovens usually have a light in or near the dial which lights up when the oven has been turned on and goes out when the required temperature has been reached. As a general rule cakes should be put into such ovens only when the lamp has gone out. During the baking process the lamp will turn on and off periodically but this only means that the thermostat is keeping the oven heat steady.

If an electric oven is used a large cake should be placed on the grid at the lowest shelf setting. If the grid has supports underneath it may be placed on the bottom of the oven. Small cakes, Stollen, Cream Puffs and cakes made of whisked egg whites are generally placed in the middle. Biscuits may be baked higher in the oven. Baking in a gas oven follows the rules given for gas ovens without a thermostat (see page 8).

Proper storage

Leave cakes in the tin for ten minutes after removing them from the oven then turn onto a cake wire. Cakes baked on a baking sheet should be removed from it while still warm otherwise the moisture from the cake condensing against the tin can affect the taste of the cake unfavourably. Biscuits should be removed from the sheet after cooking and placed singly on a wire. When quite cool they will retain their crispness if stored in airtight tins. Some kinds of biscuits e.g. may need to be softened by being left unstored for a while first.

CREAMING METHOD

IMPORTANT PREPARATIONS

1. **Mix together the flour and the Backin**
   If Gustin or cocoa are among the ingredients these should also be mixed with the flour (an exception is Marble Cake). Any blancmange or custard powder should first be blended with milk and then added to the mixture.

2. **Sieve together the flour and Backin**
   Sieving loosens the flour and distributes the Backin evenly through it. This makes for a light texture.

3. **Prepare the dried fruit or nuts as follows:**
   a) Wash currants and raisins thoroughly in warm water. Drain well or dry in a cloth.
   b) Hazelnuts should be finely chopped or ground according to the recipe.
   c) Almonds may be blanched by tipping them into boiling water; remove the water from heat, leave for two or three minutes then drain and remove skins. The almonds may then be chopped or ground.
   d) Candied peel should be finely diced or cut into strips.

4. **Grease the tin by brushing with softened butter or margarine.**
   The tin may also be dusted with fine breadcrumbs. N.B. Grease only the base of round cake tins.

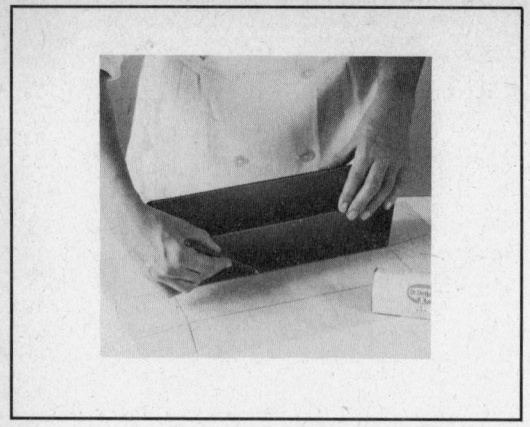

Loaf tins may be lined with paper — this means that the cake is more easily removed from the tin after baking and it will also keep fresh longer. Place the tin on the paper and draw round the base; tip it over and draw round the side; continue thus with each side. Cut out the corners and crease the base lines.

CAKE MIXING METHOD

Cream the fat (butter, margarine or lard) and gradually add to it the sugar, vanillin sugar, eggs and flavourings. Mix and sieve together the flour and Backin and add to the creamed ingredients alternately with the milk. Use only so much milk as to give a firm dropping consistency. Fold in any dried fruit prepared according to the recipe and fill the mixture into the prepared tin.

EIGHT SIMPLE STEPS

1. "Cream the fat (butter, margarine or lard) . . . ."

It is important that the fat should be neither liquid nor too firm. Liquid fat cannot be creamed successfully and hard fat must be softened first. To do this, rinse out the mixing bowl with hot

water, then work the fat well through with a mixing spoon (preferably with a hole in it). Grip the spoon handle as far down as possible and hold it vertically in the bowl (the bowl should be of earthenware or china with a rounded base) and stir in an anti-clockwise direction. The fat is sufficiently creamed when it hangs on the spoon in points when this is held up.

2. "... and gradually add to it the sugar, vanillin sugar, ..."

Sugar and vanillin sugar should be added a tablespoon at a time to the creamed fat. Beat until the sugar is well mixed in and use fine sugar rather than coarse as it is more easily absorbed.

3. "... eggs, ..."

Break each egg into a cup first to ensure that it is fresh. Newer add all the eggs at once; each egg should be well beaten in before the next is added. The cake mixture should by now look smooth and no sugar grains should be visible.

4. "... and flavourings. ..."

After the eggs have been added mix in the flavourings (baking essence, etc).

5. **"Mix and sieve together the flour and Backin and add to the creamed ingredients alternately with milk...."**

   Mix in two or three heaped tablespoons of flour at a time and add a little milk when the mixture becomes too firm. The flour-Backin mixture should be thoroughly absorbed before milk is added because any direct contact between Backin and liquid should be avoided, otherwise the rising agent would be activated too early and be thus lost. When all the flour and milk have been added beat briefly to ensure even rising and "mixing bubbles".

6. **"Use only so much milk as to give a firm dropping consistency"...**

   The exact amount of milk can never be given as this depends on the absorbency of the flour and the size of the eggs. The mixture has the right consistency when it falls heavily from the spoon. Too much milk might spoil the cake and cause "water hollows", so the mixture should on no account be thin enough to run off the spoon. An exception to this rule are cake mixtures containing more fat and eggs than usual; here the liquid is comprised of eggs and this will become firm during cooking.

7. **"Fold in any dried fruit prepared according to the recipe..."**

   The dried fruit should not be

mixed in vigorously but should be folded in gently so that the currants and sultanas do not become bruised and discolour the cake mixture.

8. "... fill the mixture into the prepared tin."
Fill the finished cake mixture into the prepared tin or mould, using a plastic scraper if possible, and stroke it even with a fork.
The tin or mould should be two-thirds full of cake mixture.

BAKING CAKES MADE BY THE CREAMING METHOD

All cakes should be baked according to the instructions in the recipe. Before removing from the oven test to see if the cake is done by piercing the middle with a wooden cocktail stick; if this comes away clean the cake is done. Remove from the oven and leave to stand for five or ten minutes then turn out onto a cake wire so that it can dry off. If a round cake tin is used loosen from the sides first with a knife.

CAKES IN BAKING TINS

Marble Cake

Cake mixture:
9 oz. (250 g) butter or margarine
9 oz. (250 g) sugar
1 packet Oetker Vanillin Sugar
3–4 eggs
a pinch of salt
1 bottle Oetker rum flavour
1 1/8 lb. (500 g) plain flour
1 packet Oetker Baking Powder Backin
about 1/5 pt. (115 ccm) milk
3 level tbsp. cocoa
a well heaped tbsp. sugar
2–3 tbsp. milk

For the cake mixture, cream the fat and gradually add to it the sugar, vanillin sugar, eggs and flavourings. Mix and sieve together the flour and Backin and add to the creamed ingredients alternately with the milk, but use only as much milk as to give a firm dropping consistency. Grease a ring or loaf baking tin and dust with breadcrumbs. Fill 2/3 of the mixture into the tin. Add the sieved cocoa and the sugar to the remaining 1/3 mixture, and mix with enough of the milk to give again a firm dropping consistency. Spread the dark mixture over the light, then draw a fork down and round through both mixtures and swirl the two together.
Oven: moderately hot.
Baking time: 50–65 minutes.

Fruity Filled Ring

Cake mixture:
3½ oz. (100 g) butter or margarine
5½ oz. (150 g) sugar
1 packet Oetker Vanillin Sugar
3 eggs
pinch of salt
4 drops Oetker Baking Essence, lemon flavour
5½ oz. (150 g) plain flour
5 slightly heaped tbsp. Oetker Gustin (corn starch powder)
2 level tsp. (6 g) Oetker Baking Powder Backin

Cream filling:
1 packet Oetker Marimba, mandarine flavour
3½ oz. (100 g) sugar
¾ pt. (425 ccm) and 5 tbsp. water
7 oz. (200 g) butter or margarine

Nut caramel coating:
a knob of butter
2 oz. (60 g) sugar
4½ oz. (125 g) blanched and chopped almonds

For decorating (if desired):
mandarine segments

For the cake mixture, cream the fat and gradually add to it the sugar, vanillin sugar, eggs and flavourings. Mix and sieve together the flour, Gustin and Backin and stir into the mixture a tablespoon at a time. Fill the mixture into a greased ring tin.
Oven: moderately hot.
Baking time: 35–45 minutes.

For the cream, mix the contents of the two bags in the Marimba packet with the sugar in a small basin; blend with 6 tbsp. of the water. Bring the rest of the water to the boil, remove from heat and mix in the blended Marimba mixture. Heat up once more, stirring all the time; boil briefly and leave to cool, stirring now and again to prevent a skin forming. Cream the butter or margarine and beat in the cooled Marimba, a spoonful at a time (take care that neither butter nor Marimba is too cool or the cream may curdle).

For the nut caramel coating, melt the butter and sugar and heat, stirring all the time until the sugar is lightly browned. Add the chopped almonds and stir further over heat until the nut caramel is sufficiently browned. Turn onto an oiled plate to cool and when quite cold crush into small pieces.

Cut the cooled cake through twice and fill with cream. Sandwich together and coat the outside with cream, reserving a little. Sprinkle with the nut caramel, decorate generously with mandarine segments and the rest of the cream.

Gustin Cake

Cake mixture:
9 oz. (250 g) butter or margarine
7 oz. (200 g) sugar
1 packet Oetker Vanillin Sugar
3 eggs
a pinch of salt
½ bottle Oetker Baking Essence, lemon flavour
13 oz. (370 g) plain flour
4½ oz. (125 g) Oetker Gustin (corn starch powder)
1 packet Oetker Baking Powder Backin
⅕ pt. (115 ccm) milk

For the cake mixture, cream the fat and gradually add to it the sugar, vanillin sugar, eggs and the flavouring. Mix and sieve together the flour, Gustin and Backin and add to the mixture alternately with the milk, but use only as much milk as to give a firm dropping consistency. Grease a ring baking tin and dust with breadcrumbs. Fill the mixture into it.
Oven: moderately hot.
Baking time: 50–60 minutes.

Frankfurt Ring (Phot. page 146)

Cake mixture:
3½ oz. (100 g) butter or margarine
5½ oz. (150 g) sugar
3 eggs
a pinch of salt
4 drops Oetker Baking Essence, lemon flavour or ½ bottle Oetker rum flavour
5½ oz. (150 g) plain flour
1¾ oz. (50 g) Oetker Gustin (corn starch powder)
2 level tsp. (6 g) Oetker Baking Powder Backin

Butter cream filling:
1 packet Oetker Pudding Powder, vanilla flavour
3½ oz. (100 g) sugar
5 tbsp. cold milk
7 oz. (200 g) butter or margarine

Nut caramel coating topping:
1 knob of butter
3 slightly heaped tbsp. sugar (about 2½ oz. (70 g))
4½ oz. (125 g) almonds (blanched and finely chopped) or hazelnuts (finely chopped)

For the cake mixture, cream the fat and gradually add to it the sugar, eggs and flavouring. Mix and sieve together the flour, Gustin and Backin and stir them in a tablespoon at a time. Fill the mixture into a greased ring tin and bake low in the oven.

For the filling, blend the pudding powder and the sugar with the 5 tbsp. milk. Bring the ¾ pt. milk to the boil, remove from heat and stir in the prepared pudding powder. Bring to the boil again, then cool, stirring fairly frequently to prevent a skin forming. Cream the fat and add the pudding, a tablespoon at a time. Take care that neither pudding nor fat is too cold, otherwise the cream will curdle.

For the topping, melt the butter and sugar together and stir till the sugar begins to turn a light brown. Add the nuts and reheat, stirring all the time until the caramel is brown. Pour it on an oiled plate to cool. When cold, pound it into small pieces. Cut the cake through twice and spread with cream filling, saving enough to coat on the outside of the cake, sprinkle with the nut caramel and decorate with the rest of the cream. This cake tastes best, when eaten the day after it is filled.

Oven: moderately hot.
Baking time: 35–45 minutes.

Extra Fine Ring Cake

Cake mixture:
9 oz. (250 g) butter or margarine
11 oz. (310 g) sugar
6 eggs
a pinch of salt
3 drops Oetker Baking Essence, lemon flavour
11 oz. (310 g) plain flour
3½ oz. (100 g) Oetker Gustin (corn starch powder)
3 level tsp. (9 g) Oetker Baking Powder Backin
7 oz. (200 g) almonds (blanched and ground)

For the cake mixture, cream the fat and gradually add to it the sugar, eggs and flavourings. Mix and sieve together the flour, Gustin and Backin and add a tablespoon at a time to the creamed ingredients. Finally fold in the almonds. Grease a ring baking tin and dust it with breadcrumbs. Fill the cake mixture into it.

Oven: moderately hot.
Baking time: 50–60 minutes.

Orange Cake   Recipe page 24

Rodon Cake

Cake mixture: large quantity
7 oz. (200 g) butter or margarine
7 oz. (200 g) sugar
1 packet Oetker Vanillin Sugar
4 eggs
a pinch of salt
1 1/8 lb. (500 g) plain flour
1 packet Oetker Baking Powder Backin
about 1/5 pt. (115 ccm) milk
5 1/2 oz. (150 g) currants
  (washed and well drained)
5 1/2 oz. (150 g) sultanas
  (washed and well drained)

Chocolate icing:
7 oz. (200 g) icing sugar
3 level tbsp. hot water
1 oz. (30 g) melted coconut butter

Cake mixture: small quantity
1 3/4 oz. (50 g) butter or margarine
1 3/4 oz. (50 g) sugar
1 packet Oetker Vanillin Sugar
1 egg
a pinch of salt
4 1/2 oz. (125 g) plain flour
1 slightly heaped tsp. Oetker Baking
  Powder Backin
about 3 tbsp. milk
1 1/2 oz. (45 g) currants
  (washed and well drained)
1 1/2 oz. (45 g) sultanas
  (washed and well drained)

For dusting:
a little icing sugar

For the cake mixture, cream the fat and gradually add to it the sugar, vanillin sugar, eggs or egg and salt. Mix and sieve together the flour and Backin and add to the mixture alternately with the milk, but use only as much milk as to give a firm dropping consistency. Finally fold in the currants and sultanas. Grease a ring baking tin and dust with breadcrumbs. Fill the mixture into the tin.

For the icing, sieve together the icing sugar and cocoa and blend with sufficient water to give a thick coating consistency. Stir in the hot fat, then spread over the cold cake. Or dust with icing sugar.

Oven: moderate.
Baking time: 50–65 minutes.

Apple or Cherry Sponge Cake (Phot. page 91)

Cake mixture:
3½–4½ oz. (100–125 g) butter or margarine
4½ oz. (125 g) sugar
2–3 eggs
a pinch of salt
4 drops Oetker Baking Essence, lemon flavour
7 oz. (200 g) plain flour
2 level tsp. (6 g) Oetker Baking Powder Backin
1–4 tbsp. milk

For the fruit topping:
about 1½ lb. (680 g) apples
or 1¾ lb. (790 g) morello cherries

For dusting:
a little icing sugar

For the cake mixture, cream the fat and gradually add to it the sugar, eggs and flavourings. Mix and sieve together the flour and the Backin and add, a tablespoon at a time, to the creamed ingredients. As the mixture becomes firmer, add the milk, but use only so much milk as to give a firm dropping consistency. Fill the mixture into a well-greased round cake tin (10½ in. in diameter, with a removable rim).

For the topping, peel the apples and cut into quarters. Make a number of shallow slits on the back of the quarters, lengthways, and lay them on the mixture; or wash and stone the cherries and lay them on the mixture.

Oven: moderately hot.

Baking time: 40–50 minutes.

Dust the cooled cake with icing sugar.

Sand Cake

Cake mixture:
9 oz. (250 g) butter or margarine
7 oz. (200 g) castor sugar
1 packet Oetker Vanillin Sugar
4 eggs
a pinch of salt
a few drops of Oetker Baking Essence, lemon flavour or ½ bottle Oetker rum flavour
4½ oz. (125 g) plain flour
4½ oz. (125 g) Oetker Gustin (corn starch powder)
½ level tsp. (1½ g) Oetker Baking Powder Backin

Icing:
4½ oz. (125 g) icing sugar
3 level tbsp. cocoa
1–2 tbsp. hot water
1 oz. (30 g) coconut butter, melted (optional)

For the cake mixture, melt the fat and cool until slightly firm. Add the sugar and vanillin sugar and beat until white and fluffy. Gradually add eggs (beat in each egg for five minutes before adding the next) and flavourings. Mix and sieve together the flour, the Gustin and Backin and add to the creamed ingredients, a tablespoon at a time. Grease a long loaf cake tin and line with paper. Fill the mixture into it.

Oven: moderately hot.

Baking time: 60–75 minutes.

For the icing, sieve the icing sugar with the cocoa and blend with enough water to give a thick coating consistency. Stir in the melted fat, if desired. Brush or spread over the cooled cake.

Iced Ring Cake

Nut caramel:
a knob of butter
1³/₄ oz. (50 g) (2 well heaped tbsp.) sugar
3¹/₂ oz. (100 g) almonds
(blanched and finely chopped)
or
hazelnuts
(blanched and finely chopped)

Cake mixture:
3¹/₂ oz. (100 g) butter or margarine
5¹/₂ oz. (150 g) sugar
3 eggs
a pinch of salt
¹/₂ bottle Oetker rum flavour
5¹/₂ oz. (150 g) plain flour
2¹/₂ oz. (70 g) Oetker Gustin
(corn starch powder)
2 level tsp. (3 g) Oetker Baking Powder Backin
1³/₄–3¹/₂ oz. (50–100 g) plain chocolate coffee beans

Icing:
7 oz. (200 g) icing sugar
1 well heaped tsp. instant coffee powder
about 2 tbsp. hot water

For decorating:
a few chocolate coffee beans

For the nut caramel, melt the butter and sugar together and stir until the sugar begins to turn a light brown. Add the nuts and reheat, stirring all the time until the caramel is brown. Place it on an oiled plate to cool. When cold, crush it into small pieces.

For the cake mixture, cream the fat and gradually add to it the sugar, eggs and flavourings. Mix and sieve together the flour, Gustin and Backin, and add gradually to the creamed ingredients. Mix in the halved chocolate beans. Grease a ring baking tin and fill the mixture into it.

Oven: moderately hot.
Baking time: 35–40 minutes.

For the icing, sieve the icing sugar and mix with the instant coffee powder. Blend with sufficient water to give a thick coating consistency. Brush over the cooled cake and decorate with chocolate beans.

Nut Cake

9 oz. (250 g) butter or margarine
7 oz. (200 g) sugar
4 eggs
2–3 drops Oetker Baking Essence, bitter almond flavour
9 oz. (250 g) plain flour
3 level tsp. Oetker Baking Powder Backin
9 oz. (250 g) hazelnuts (ground)
1³/₄ oz. (50 g) chocolate
(finely chopped)

For dusting:
a little icing sugar

For the cake mixture, cream the fat and gradually add to it the sugar, eggs and the flavouring. Mix and sieve together the flour and Backin and add to the mixture, together with the nuts, a tablespoonful at a time. Finally fold in the chocolate. Grease a ring baking tin and fill the mixture into it.

Oven: moderately hot.
Baking time: 50–65 minutes.
Dust the cooled cake with icing sugar.

Gooseberry Cake

Cake mixture:
4½ oz. (125 g) butter or margarine
4½ oz. (125 g) sugar
1 packet Oetker Vanillin Sugar
2 eggs
pinch of salt
3½ oz. (100 g) plain flour
1 oz. (30 g) (3 slightly heaped tbsp.) Oetker Gustin (corn starch powder)
½ level tsp. (1½ g) Oetker Baking Powder Backin

Butter cream filling:
½ packet Oetker Pudding Powder, vanilla flavour
1¾ oz. (50 g) sugar
½ pt. (285 ccm) cold milk
3½ oz. (125 g) butter or margarine
2 tbsp. lemon juice

Fruit topping:
Bottled or canned gooseberries (1 l size)

Glaze:
1 packet Oetker Cake Glaze, transparent and sugar quantity according to packet

For decorating:
1¾ oz. (50 g) almonds, blanched and chopped

For the cake mixture, cream the fat and gradually add the sugar, vanillin sugar, eggs and salt. Mix and sieve together the flour, Backin and Gustin and add these to the cake mixture, a tbsp. at a time. Divide the cake mixture into three equal quantities and spread each onto the base of a greased cake tin with a removable rim diameter about 10 in. (26 cm). Bake each layer without the rim until golden brown.

Oven: moderately hot.

Baking time: about 10 minutes.

Remove the layers from the tin immediately after baking and cool on a cake wire.

For the butter cream filling, blend the pudding powder and sugar with 3 tbsp. of the milk. Bring the rest of the milk to the boil; remove from heat, stir in the blended pudding powder mixture and boil up briefly. Stir occasionally while cooling.

Cream the fat and beat in the pudding, a tbsp. at a time, taking care that neither fat nor pudding are too cool otherwise the cream may curdle. Finally add the lemon juice, beating in well. Sandwich together the three layers with ⅔ of the cream, leaving the top layer surface free of cream.

For the fruit topping, drain the gooseberries well on a sieve and measure off ½ pt. (285 ccm) of the juice or syrup. Arrange the fruit on top of the cake leaving a 1 in. (2 cm) wide border free round the circumference. Prepare the cake glaze according to the instructions on the packet and spoon over the gooseberries.

For the border, roast the almonds lightly on a tin in the oven, turning frequently until golden brown. Coat the border and the sides of the cake with some of the remaining butter cream and pipe the rest of the cream onto the border around the fruit. Sprinkle the cream with the cooled almonds.

Empress Frederick Cake

Cake mixture:
9 oz. (250 g) coconut butter
　or 11 oz. (310 g) margarine
11 oz. (310 g) sugar
1 packet Oetker Vanillin Sugar
5 eggs
1 egg yolk
$1/2$ egg white
3 drops Oetker Baking Essence,
　bitter almond flavour
$1/2$ bottle Oetker rum flavour
a pinch of salt
11 oz. (310 g) plain flour
$2^{1}/_{2}$ oz. (70 g) Oetker Gustin
　(corn starch powder)
2 level tsp. (6 g) Oetker Baking
　Powder Backin
$4^{1}/_{2}$ oz. (125 g) candied lemon peel
　(finely chopped)

Icing:
6 oz. (170 g) icing sugar
$1/2$ egg white
about 3 tbsp. lemon juice
$1^{3}/_{4}$ oz. (50 g) candied lemon peel
　(cut into small cubes or strips)

For the cake mixture, either melt the coconut butter and cool until slightly firm or cream the margarine, add the sugar and vanillin sugar and beat until white and fluffy. Gradually add the eggs, egg yolk, $1/2$ egg white and flavourings. Mix and sieve together the flour, Gustin and Backin and add to the mixture a tablespoon at a time. Fold in the candied lemon peel. Grease a round cake tin with a removable rim (diameter $10^{1}/_{2}$ in.). Fill the mixture into it.
Oven: moderately hot.
Baking time: 65–75 minutes.
For the icing, sieve the icing sugar and blend with the egg white and enough lemon juice to give a thick coating consistency. Brush over the cooled cake and decorate with the candied lemon peel.

Orange Cake (Phot. page 18)

Cake mixture:
7 oz. (200 g) butter or margarine
7 oz. (200 g) sugar
1 packet Oetker Vanillin Sugar
3 eggs
a pinch of salt
9 oz. (250 g) plain flour
$4^{1}/_{2}$ oz. (125 g) Oetker Gustin
　(corn starch powder)
4 level tsp. (12 g) Oetker Baking Powder
　Backin
about 4 tbsp. milk

For sprinkling on the cake after baking:
about $1/2$ pt. (285 ccm) orange juice
juice of half a lemon

For the cake mixture, cream the fat and gradually add to it the sugar, vanillin sugar, eggs and salt. Mix and sieve together the flour, Gustin and Backin, and add to the creamed ingredients alternately with the milk, but use only as much milk as to give a firm dropping consistency. Grease a long loaf baking tin and line with paper. Fill the mixture into it.
Oven: moderately hot.
Baking time: 50–70 minutes.
When the cake has cooled, pierce the top a number of times with a wooden cocktail stick. Mix together the orange and lemon juice, and sprinkle or brush it on the cake. Leave time for the juice to become absorbed.

Prince Regent Cake (Phot. page 17)

Cake mixture:
9 oz. (250 g) butter or margarine
9 oz. (250 g) sugar
1 packet Oetker Vanillin Sugar
4 eggs
a pinch of salt
7 oz. (200 g) plain flour
1¾ oz. (50 g) Oetker Gustin
  (corn starch powder)
1 level tsp. (3 g) Oetker Baking
  Powder Backin

Butter cream filling:
1 packet Oetker Gala Chocolate
  Pudding Powder
1 level tsp. cocoa
3½ oz. (100 g) sugar
5 tbsp. cold milk
1¾ oz. (50 g) coconut butter
  (optional)
¾ pt. (425 ccm) milk
9 oz. (250 g) butter or margarine

Icing:
5½ oz. (150 g) icing sugar
3 level tbsp. cocoa
2–3 tbsp. hot water
¾ oz. (20 g) butter or coconut butter
  (melted)

For the cake mixture, cream the fat and add to it the sugar, vanillin sugar, eggs and salt. Mix and sieve together the flour, Gustin and Backin and add to the creamed ingredients, a tablespoon at a time. Bake 8 separate layers out of the mixture. Spread almost 2 tbsp. of mixture each time on the base of a well greased round cake tin (with removable rim and of 10½ in. diameter). Take care that the mixture is not too thin near the edge as it might become brown. Bake each layer without the cake tin rim until golden. Cool each layer on a cake wire after baking.
Oven: moderately hot.
Baking time: about 8–10 minutes.
For the filling, blend the pudding powder, cocoa, and the sugar with the 5 tbsp. milk. Bring the ¾ pt. (425 ccm) milk to the boil, remove from heat, stir in the pudding powder mixture and bring to the boil once more, stirring all the time. If coconut butter is used, add this to the hot pudding. Set aside to cool, stirring frequently to prevent a skin forming.
Cream the fat and beat in the cold pudding gradually (take care that neither pudding nor fat are too cool or the butter cream may curdle). Spread each layer with the filling and place on top of one another to build the cake, the top layer being without filling.
For the icing, sieve the icing sugar with the cocoa and add sufficient hot water to give a good coating consistency. Add the hot fat and ice the cake.

Fruit Flan (Phot. page 90)

Cake mixture:
2½ oz. (70 g) butter or margarine
2½ oz. (70 g) sugar
1 packet Oetker Vanillin Sugar
2 eggs
a pinch of salt
5½ oz. (150 g) plain flour
1 level tsp. (3 g) Oetker Baking
  Powder Backin
about 2 tbsp. milk

Custard and fruit topping:
1 packet Oetker Sauce Powder,
  vanilla flavour

For the cake mixture, cream the fat and gradually add to it the sugar, vanillin sugar, eggs and salt. Mix and sieve together the flour and Backin and add to the creamed ingredients alternately with the milk, but use only as much milk as will give a firm dropping consistency. Grease a large flan tin (10½ in. diameter) and dust with breadcrumbs. Fill the cake mixture into the flan tin and smooth it level.
Oven: moderately hot.
Baking time: 20–25 minutes.
For the custard and fruit topping, mix the sauce powder with the sugar, stir in a little cold milk and gradually add the rest. Bring to the boil, stirring all the

Continued on next page

1 well heaped tbsp. sugar
1/4 pt. (140 ccm) and 6 tbsp. cold milk
about 1 1/2 lb. (680 g) raw, stewed,
    tinned or bottled (apples, apricots,
    strawberries, cherries, peaches,
    gooseberries, etc.)

Glaze:
1 packet Oetker Cake Glaze, transparent
almost 1/2 pt. (285 ccm) water or fruit juice
sugar according to the directions on
the packet

For decorating:
a few almonds or hazelnuts (sliced)

time. Set aside to cool, stirring now and again. When cool, spread evenly over the base of the flan case.
Soft fruits, such as apricots, strawberries and peaches should be left uncooked. They should be washed and well drained, stoned or cleaned.
Hard fruits, e.g. apples, should be peeled and cored, cut into quarters or eighths and poached in syrup. Drain well. Bottled or tinned fruit should be well drained.
Arrange the prepared fruit on the custard on the flan case. Make the cake glaze according to the directions on the packet. Pour onto the fruit and decorate around the edge with the sliced nuts.

Layer Cake

Cake mixture:
9 oz. (250 g) butter or margarine
9 oz. (250 g) sugar
1 packet Oetker Vanillin Sugar
2 eggs
4 egg yolks
1–2 tbsp. rum
5 1/2 oz. (150 g) plain flour
3 1/2 oz. (100 g) Oetker Gustin
    (corn starch powder)
3 level tsp. (9 g) Oetker Baking
    Powder Backin
4 egg whites

Icing:
6 oz. (170 g) icing sugar
2–3 tbsp. hot water
a largish knob of butter (melted)

For the cake mixture, cream the fat and gradually add to it the sugar, vanillin sugar, 2 eggs, the 4 egg yolks and the rum. Mix and sieve together the flour, Gustin and Backin and add gradually to the creamed ingredients. Beat the 4 egg whites until stiff and fold in carefully.
Line a round cake tin with removable rim (diameter 10 1/2 in.) with paper. Spread almost 2 tablespoons of the cake mixture on the base of the tin. Smooth it flat and bake.
Oven: moderately hot.
Baking time: about 10 minutes.
Spread almost 2 tablespoons of cake mixture onto the baked layer to form the second layer. The second layer and the ones following should be baked for 8–10 minutes. Reduce heat after the second layer; if possible turn off the bottom heat or place a baking sheet or a dish with water under the cake tin. When finished the cake should have at least 8 layers.
For the icing, sieve the icing sugar and blend with enough water to give a thick coating consistency. Add the hot liquid butter and spread over the cake.
For black and white icing, take away a tablespoon of the white icing and stir into it 1 tablespoon cocoa (may need a little water). Pipe this in a spiral pattern onto the iced cake, then draw a skewer through the icing, from edge to middle and back in pattern (work quickly while both icings are wet!).

Apple Crumble Cake

Cake mixture:
7 oz. (200 g) butter or margarine
7 oz. (200 g) sugar
1 packet Oetker Vanillin Sugar
1 egg
a pinch of salt
1 1/8 lb. (500 g) plain flour
1 packet Oetker Baking Powder Backin
3 slightly heaped tbsp. breadcrumbs
Filling:
1 3/4 lb. (790 g) apples
1 packet Oetker Vanillin Sugar
sugar to taste

For the cake mixture, cream the fat and gradually add to it the sugar, vanillin sugar, egg and salt. Mix and sieve together the flour and Backin, and add half to the creamed ingredients gradually, a tablespoon at a time. Empty the rest of the flour onto the mixture and rub in with finger tips, or work in with two forks until it is crumbly.

For the filling, peel and slice the apples, mix them with the vanillin sugar and sugar according to taste. (If the apples are hard, stew until half done with the vanillin sugar and the sugar in very little water; then cool.)

Grease a round cake tin with a removable rim (10 1/2 in. in a diameter). Fill half the cake mixture into it, pressing it flat on the bottom and slightly higher against the sides. Sprinkle with the breadcrumbs. Fill the apples on top, leaving 3/8 in. free round the edge. Empty the rest of the crumble mixture onto the apples and press lightly inside the rim.

Oven: moderately hot.
Baking time: 45–55 minutes.

Spicy Ring

Cake mixture:
6 oz. (170 g) butter or margarine
8 oz. (225 g) sugar
1 packet Oetker Vanillin Sugar
4 eggs
a pinch of salt
1/2 level tsp. ground cloves
pinch of nutmeg
1 level tsp. ground cinnamon
10 1/2 oz. (300 g) plain flour
1 packet Oetker Gala Chocolate Pudding Powder
4 level tsp. (12 g) Oetker Baking Powder Backin
3 1/2 oz. (100 g) grated chocolate
1–2 tbsp. milk
For dusting:
a little icing sugar

Cream the fat and gradually add to it the sugar, vanillin sugar, eggs and spices. Mix and sieve together the flour, pudding powder and Backin and add to the creamed ingredients, a tablespoon at a time. If the mixture becomes too firm, add the milk. Grease a ring baking tin and fill the cake mixture into it.

Oven: moderately hot.
Baking time: 50–60 minutes.
Dust the cooled cake with icing sugar.

Rehrücken

Cake mixture:
3½ oz. (100 g) butter or margarine
5½ oz. (150 g) sugar
4 eggs
3½ oz. (100 g) grated chocolate
1¾ oz. (50 g) plain flour
2 packets Oetker Chocolate Pudding Powder
1½ level tsp. (4½ g) Oetker Baking Powder Backin
about 2 tsp. milk
2½ oz. (70 g) ground almonds
Icing:
4½ oz. (125 g) icing sugar
3 level tbsp. cocoa
about 1½ tbsp. hot water
¾ oz. (20 g) melted coconut butter (optional)
For decorating:
1¾ oz. (50 g) almonds, blanched and cut into longish spikes

For the cake mixture, cream the fat and gradually add to it the sugar, eggs and grated chocolate. Mix and sieve together the flour, pudding powder and Backin, and stir in alternately with the milk, but use only as much milk as will give a firm dropping consistency. Finally fold in the ground almonds. Grease a small loaf cake tin, if possible with a rounded base. Fill the cake mixture into it.
Oven: moderately hot.
Baking time: 50–60 minutes.
For the icing, sieve the icing sugar with the cocoa and blend with as much water as will give a good coating consistency. Add the hot fat and ice the cake. Stick in the pieces of almonds as spikes.

King's Cake

Cake mixture:
9 oz. (250 g) butter or margarine
7 oz. (200 g) sugar
1 packet Oetker Vanillin Sugar
5 eggs
a pinch of salt
½ bottle Oetker Baking Essence, lemon flavour or 1 bottle Oetker rum flavour
1⅛ lb. (500 g) plain flour
4 level tsp. (12 g) Oetker Baking Powder Backin
5–8 tbsp. milk
5½ oz. (150 g) currants (washed and well drained)
9 oz. (250 g) raisins (washed and well drained)
4½ oz. (125 g) candied lemon peel (finely chopped)

Cream the fat and gradually add to it the sugar, vanillin sugar, eggs and flavourings. Mix and sieve together the flour and Backin and add to the creamed ingredients alternately with the milk, but use only as much milk as will give a firm dropping consistency. Finally fold in the dried fruit and candied lemon peel. Grease a long loaf baking tin and line with paper. Fill the cake mixture into it.
Oven: moderately hot.
Baking time: 80–100 minutes.

Ottilia Cake

Cake mixture: large quantity
9 oz. (250 g) butter or margarine
7 oz. (200 g) sugar
1 packet Oetker Vanillin Sugar
4 eggs
a pinch of salt
½ bottle Oetker rum flavour
7 oz. (200 g) plain flour
1¾ oz. (50 g) Oetker Gustin
   (corn starch powder)
1 level tsp. (3 g) Oetker Baking
   Powder Backin
3½ oz. (100 g) ground almonds
2½ oz. (70 g) plain chocolate
   (finely chopped)
¾ oz. (50 g) candied lemon peel
   (diced)

Cake mixture: small quantity
3½ oz. (100 g) butter or margarine
2½ oz. (70 g) sugar
1 packet Oetker Vanillin Sugar
1 egg
a pinch of salt
5 drops Oetker rum flavour
3½ oz. (100 g) plain flour
1 oz. (30 g) Oetker Gustin
   (corn starch powder)
½ level tsp. (1½ g) Oetker Baking
   Powder Backin
1½ oz. (45 g) ground almonds
¾ oz. (20 g) plain chocolate
   (finely chopped)
½ oz. (15 g) candied lemon peel
   (diced)

For dusting:
a little icing sugar

For the cake mixture, cream the fat and gradually add to it the sugar, vanillin sugar, eggs and flavourings. Mix and sieve together the flour, Gustin and Backin and add to the creamed ingredients, a tablespoon at a time. Lastly carefully fold in the almonds, the chocolate and the candied peel. Grease a long loaf cake tin and line it with paper. Fill mixture into it.
Oven: moderately hot.
Baking time: 65–75 minutes.
Dust the cooled cake with icing sugar.

CAKES ON A BAKING SHEET

Crumble Cake with Cottage Cheese Filling

Cake mixture:
9 oz. (250 g) butter or margarine
7 oz. (200 g) sugar
1 packet Oetker Vanillin Sugar
1 egg
a pinch of salt
1 1/8 lb. (500 g) plain flour
1 packet Oetker Baking Powder Backin
Filling:
2 1/4 lb. (1000 g) cottage cheese
  (well pressed out)
1 packet Oetker Sauce Powder,
  vanilla flavour
1 egg
7 oz. (200 g) sugar
5 drops Oetker Baking Essence,
  lemon flavour
1 3/4 oz. (50 g) sultanas (washed and
  well drained)

For the cake mixture, cream the fat and gradually add to it the sugar, vanillin sugar, egg and salt. Mix and sieve together the flour and Backin and add half to the creamed ingredients, a tablespoon at a time. Empty the rest of the flour onto the mixture and rub in with the fingertips, or work in with two forks, until a crumbly mass is obtained.

For the filling, rub the cottage cheese through a fine sieve and mix with the sauce powder, egg, sugar, lemon flavouring and sultanas.

Distribute half the cake mixture evenly over a greased baking sheet. Press it flat against the base and slightly higher against the sides. Spread the cottage cheese filling evenly over the cake mixture and sprinkle the rest of the crumble over the filling.

Oven: pre-heat for 5 minutes at very hot,
           bake at moderately hot.
Baking time: 25–45 minutes.

Iced Nut Cake

Cake mixture:
9 oz. (250 g) ground hazelnuts
7 oz. (200 g) sugar
1 packet Oetker Vanillin Sugar
2–3 drops Oetker Baking Essence,
  bitter almond flavour
9 oz. (250 g) plain flour
4 level tsp. (12 g) Oetker Baking
  Powder Backin
2 eggs
1/4 pt. (140 ccm) milk
Icing:
7 oz. (200 g) icing sugar
1 heaped tsp. instant coffee powder
2–3 tbsp. hot water
3/4 oz. (20 g) butter (melted)

For the cake mixture, place all the dry ingredients in a mixing bowl, and gradually add to them the eggs and the milk. Use only as much milk as will give a firm dropping consistency. Spread the cake mixture onto a greased baking sheet, smoothing evenly.

Oven: moderately hot.
Baking time: about 25 minutes.

For the icing, sieve together the icing sugar and instant coffee powder and blend with enough hot water to give a good coating consistency. Add the hot butter. Ice the cake immediately after baking and cut into pieces.

SMALL CAKES

Piped Biscuits (plain or chocolate)

Mixture for plain biscuits:
13 oz. (370 g) butter or margarine
9 oz. (250 g) sugar
2 packets Oetker Vanillin Sugar
a pinch of salt
9 oz. (250 g) plain flour
9 oz. (250 g) Oetker Gustin
   (corn starch powder)
4½ oz. (125 g) ground almonds
Icing:
3½ oz. (100 g) icing sugar
2 level tbsp. cocoa
1½ tbsp. hot water
1¾ oz. (50 g) butter (melted)
Mixture for chocolate biscuits:
13 oz. (370 g) butter or margarine
9 oz. (250 g) sugar
1 packet Oetker Vanillin Sugar
1 tbsp. water
a pinch of salt
9 oz. (250 g) plain flour
9 oz. (250 g) Oetker Gustin
   (corn starch powder)
3 level tbsp. cocoa
4½ oz. (125 g) ground almonds

For the cake mixture, cream the fat and gradually add to it the sugar, vanillin sugar and salt (for the chocolate biscuit mixture add the water, too). Mix and sieve together the flour and Gustin (and cocoa for the chocolate biscuits mixture) and add to the creamed ingredients, a tablespoon at a time. The mixture will become very firm before all the flour has been stirred in, so knead in the rest of the flour and the almonds lightly by hand. Using a biscuit forcer, pipe the mixture onto a baking sheet in S or ring shapes.
Oven: pre-heat for 5 minutes at very hot,
   bake at moderately hot.
Baking time: about 10 minutes.
For the icing, sieve together the icing sugar and cocoa and blend with the water. Add the hot butter. Decorate the plain biscuits with the icing, brushing it over one half of the rings and the ends of the S shapes.

Shortbread Biscuits

10 oz. (280 g) butter
9 oz. (250 g) castor sugar
1 packet Oetker Vanillin Sugar
2 tbsp. milk
13 oz. (380 g) plain flour
1 level tsp. (3 g) Oetker Baking
   Powder Backin

Melt and brown the butter, then leave to cool. When the butter is firm, cream it and gradually add the sugar, vanillin sugar and milk, beating until white and fluffy. Mix and sieve together the flour and the Backin and stir ⅔ into the creamed ingredients, a tablespoon at a time. Knead the remaining flour into the mixture with the hand until quite smooth. Shape into rolls about 1½ in. (3 cm) thick and leave in a cool place until stiff. Cut off slices about ¼ in. (½ cm) thick and place in rows on a greased baking sheet.
Bake fairly high in the oven until pale yellow.
Oven: pre-heat for 5 minutes at very hot,
   bake at moderately hot.
Baking time: 10–15 minutes.

Margaret Biscuits

Cake mixture:
3½ oz. (100 g) butter or margarine
3½ oz. (100 g) sugar
1 packet Oetker Vanillin Sugar, 1 egg
a pinch of salt
2 tbsp. water
5½ oz. (150 g) plain flour
1¾ oz. (50 g) Oetker Gustin
    (corn starch powder)
1 level tsp. (3 g) Oetker Baking
    Powder Backin
1¾ oz. (50 g) plain chocolate
    (finely chopped)

Cream the fat and gradually add to it some of the sugar, the vanillin sugar, egg, the rest of the sugar, salt and water. Mix and sieve together the flour, Gustin and Backin and add to the creamed ingredients a tablespoon at a time. Fold in the chocolate. Grease a baking sheet and, using two teaspoons, place the mixture on it in little heaps the size of a walnut, not too close together. Bake until golden brown.
Oven: pre-heat for 5 minutes at very hot,
          bake at moderately hot.
Baking time: about 15 minutes.

Coconut Cookies

4½ oz. (125 g) butter or margarine
3½ oz. (100 g) sugar
1 packet Oetker Vanillin Sugar, 1 egg
4½ oz. (125 g) plain flour
2½ oz. (70 g) Oetker Gustin
    (corn starch powder)
3 level tsp. (9 g) Oetker Baking
    Powder Backin
3½ oz. (100 g) desiccated coconut

Cream the fat, and gradually add the sugar, vanillin sugar and egg. Mix and sieve together the flour, Gustin und Backin and stir into the creamed ingredients, a little at a time. Fold in the coconut. Using 2 teaspoons, place little heaps of the mixture on a greased baking sheet.
Oven: pre-heat for 5 minutes at very hot,
          bake at moderately hot.
Baking time: about 10 minutes.

Filled Shells

Cake mixture:
9 oz. (250 g) butter or margarine
6 oz. (170 g) castor sugar
1 packet Oetker Vanillin Sugar, 1 egg
6 oz. (170 g) plain flour
6 oz. (170 g) Oetker Gustin
    (corn starch powder)
2½ oz. (70 g) ground almonds
For filling and icing:
3½ oz. (100 g) couverture chocolate
    icing
1¾ oz. (50 g) apricot jam

For the cake mixture, cream the fat and gradually add the sugar, and the vanillin sugar. Beat until white and fluffy. Sieve together the flour and the Gustin and stir into the creamed ingredients, a little at a time. Fold in the almonds. Pipe the mixture, using a bag or biscuit forcer with a largish star nozzle, in little shell shapes onto a greased baking sheet.
Oven: pre-heat for 5 minutes at very hot,
          bake at moderately hot.
Baking time: 10–15 minutes.
For the filling, melt the couverture carefully in a basin in a saucepan of water over heat, stirring all the time until it is liquid. Brush the underside of one shell with icing, stick another shell against it and press well. Pair off half the shells using couverture as filling and the other half using apricot jam. Brush the tips of the filled biscuits with couverture.

WAFFLES

Cream Waffles (Hard Waffles)

Mixture:
9 oz. (250 g) butter or margarine
3½ oz. (100 g) sugar
1 packet Oetker Vanillin Sugar
4 egg yolks
4½ oz. (125 g) plain flour
4½ oz. (125 g) Oetker Gustin
  (corn starch powder)
2 level tsp. (6 g) Oetker Baking
  Powder Backin
about ½ pt. (285 ccm) fresh double
  cream
4 egg whites
For greating: bacon rind or a little oil
For dusting: a little icing sugar

For the mixture, cream the fat and gradually add the sugar, vanillin sugar and egg yolks. Sieve together the flour, Gustin and Backin and add to the creamed ingredients alternately with the cream. Beat the egg whites till stiff and fold carefully into the mixture. Heat and grease a waffle iron, and when very hot, spoon in a small quantity of the mixture and smooth quickly. Cook on both sides until golden brown. Allow the waffles to cool singly on a cake wire, and dust with icing sugar.

Sand Waffles

Mixture:
6 oz. (170 g) coconut butter
6 oz. (170 g) castor sugar
a packet Oetker Vanillin Sugar
3–4 eggs a pinch of salt
½ bottle Oetker rum flavour
7 oz. (200 g) plain flour
1¾ oz. (50 g) Oetker Gustin
  (corn starch powder)
½ level tsp. (1½ g) Oetker
  Baking Powder Backin
For greasing: bacon rind or a little oil
For dusting: a little icing sugar

For the cake mixture, melt the coconut butter and cool until slightly firm. Cream the fat and add the sugar and vanillin sugar gradually, beating until white and fluffy. Add the eggs, beating each into the mixture for five minutes. Add the flavouring. Sieve together the flour, Gustin and Backin, and stir into the creamed ingredients, a little at a time.
Heat and grease a waffle iron and when very hot, spoon in a small quantity of the mixture and smooth quickly. Cook on both sides until golden brown. Cool singly on a cake wire, then dust with icing sugar.

Eiser Cake

Mixture*:
2½ oz. (70 g) butter or margarine
9 oz. (250 g) sugar
1 packet Oetker Vanillin Sugar
2 eggs
9 oz. (250 g) plain flour
about ⅔ pt. (375 ccm) water
For greasing:
bacon rind or a little oil
*N. B. These cakes can only be made in a special "Eiser Cake" iron.

For the mixture cream the fat, then add some of the sugar, then the vanillin sugar and the eggs and then the rest of the sugar. Sieve the flour and stir into the mixture alternately with the water. Use enough water to give a thin batter. Grease an eiser cake iron and heat it. When very hot, pour in a small quantity of butter and cook on both sides until golden brown. Remove the thin cake from the iron and roll quickly while still hot into a roll or cone. Keep crisp by storing in an airtight tin.

KNEADING METHOD

IMPORTANT PREPARATIONS

1. For the kneading process the fat must be very firm. Soft fat should be kept in a cool place for some time beforehand.
2. Dried fruits should be prepared in the same way as for Creaming Method, see page 11.
3. Baking tins and sheets need not as a rule be greased for this pastry. Exceptions are flan and tartlet cases, and baking sheets for Stollen and pastry mixtures which contain more milk or water than usual.

PASTRY MIXING METHOD

Mix and sieve together the flour and Backin onto a pastry board or cool slab. Make a well in the centre and pour in the sugar, vanillin sugar, flavourings, eggs and any liquid mentioned in the recipe. Draw in some of the flour from the sides of the well to mix with these to form a thickish paste. Add the cold fat (butter, margarine or lard) cut into small pieces and any dried fruit, prepared according to instructions. Cover the whole with more of the flour. Starting from the middle work all these ingredients quickly with the hands into a smooth firm paste. Form into a roll. If it should be sticky cool well through for some time, or add a little flour.

TEN SIMPLE STEPS

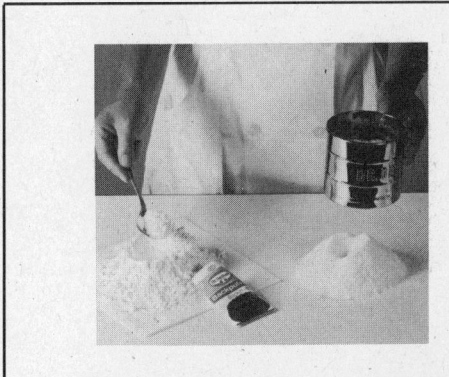

1. **Mix and sieve together the flour and Backin onto a pastry board or cool slab....**
The mixing and sieving loosens the flour and distributes the baking powder evenly throughout, thus making for lighter pastry. If cocoa is mentioned in the recipe, add this to the flour.

2. **Make a well in the centre....**
Using the back of a spoon, make a well in the middle of the heap of flour taking care that the rim has the same thickness all the way round and that the base is not too thin, on no account should the pastry board be visible through it.

Eberswalder Pastries   Recipe page 140
Berlin Pancakes   Recipe page 141
Mutzenmandeln   Recipe page 142

3. **...and pour in the sugar, vanillin sugar, flavourings, eggs and any liquid mentioned in the recipe....**

Always add the ingredients in this order, making a well in the sugar to receive the other ingredients. Eggs should first be broken into a cup, one at a time, to ensure that they are fresh before pouring into the well. Any liquid in the recipe should be poured onto the sugar. If the recipe requires more than one tablespoon, add gradually, a little at a time, working in each one before adding the next.

4. **... Draw in some of the flour from the sides of the well to mix with these to form a thickish paste....**

Work the sugar, vanillin sugar, flavourings, eggs and liquid together with some of the flour with a fork to form a thickish paste. Work in the flour quickly. It is important for the kneading later that this paste should be thick enough.

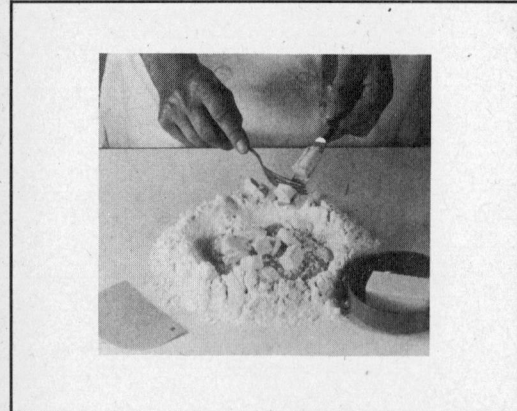

5. **... Add the cold fat (butter, margarine or lard) cut into small pieces and any dried fruit, prepared according to instructions....**

It is essential for the success of this pastry that the fat (butter, margarine or lard) is cold and firm at this stage. If the fat is soft, the pastry will become sticky and difficult to handle. Adding more flour to pastry containing more fat than usual will cause the pastry to be crumbly and hard when baked. The cutting of the fat into small pieces ensures even distribution through the pastry. Any dried fruit mentioned in the recipe should be placed on the fat.

6. . . . **Cover the whole with more of the flour.** . . .
   The fat (butter, margarine or lard) is covered with the flour to prevent it becoming softened by hand warmth during kneading.

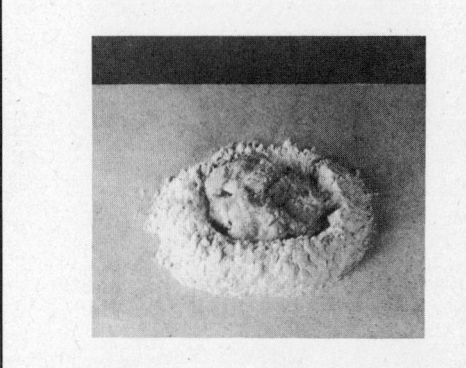

7. . . . **Starting from the middle, work all these ingredients quickly with the hands into a firm smooth paste.** . . .
   This working with the hands or kneading has three separate movements: lifting, pressing and turning (see figs. a, b, c).

a) **Lifting the pastry:**
   With fingers together and stretched, reach under the pastry, lift up one half and tip it onto the other half still lying on the board. Hold the pastry quite loosely so that it remains cool.

b) **Pressing the pastry:**
Using the part of the hand nearest the wrist, press the pastry. Do not use the whole surface of the hand or the fingers, which should be held as high as possible from the pastry.

c) **Turning the pastry:**
Place the insides of the hands against the pastry and move it through an angle of 90° towards the right. During this movement on the pastry board the pastry absorbs flour and so cannot become sticky.

Repeat these three movements in sequence until a smooth firm paste has been formed. Gather the flour together beneath the pastry now and again so that it can become absorbed.

8. .... **Form into a roll.**
If the pastry should be sticky cool well through for some time or add a little flour. . . .
The pastry is formed into a roll to facilitate rolling out. If pastry containing more fat than usual is sticky, cool well through for a while. A little flour may be added to pastry which is sticky because it contains water or milk. Clean the pastry-board or slab, removing any remnants of pastry, before rolling out the pastry, so that any sticking to the slab is avoided. Dust the slab evenly with flour.

9. In order not to spoil the quality of the pastry by too much rolling and handling, use only a small amount at a time (especially when making biscuits). During rolling out the rolling pin should really turn, and should move lightly over the pastry (do not press hard). During rolling out, draw a long blunt knife (palette knife) between the pastry and the board now and again to loosen any part that should stick.

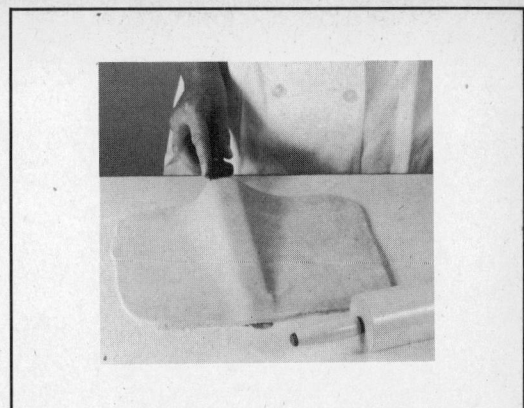

10. a) When making biscuits cut out as economically as possible. Renewed handling and rolling causes the pastry to deteriorate in quality.

b) Pastry flan cases may be baked either in a round cake tin with a removable rim, or in a special flan case tin. If a round cake tin is used, roll out $2/3$ of the pastry to fit the base of the tin; knead a level tablespoon of flour into the rest of the pastry and form into a long roll; lay this roll around the inside of the base and press it against the sides with two fingers so that it is $1^1/2$ in. (3 cm) high. Prick the base well with a fork so that air cannot gather underneath.

CAKES MADE BY THE KNEADING METHOD

Carefully follow the instructions in each recipe about the baking of pastry. Remove the cake from the tin or baking sheet right away after baking and place on a cake wire to cool. Small cakes and biscuits should be placed singly on the wire.

CAKES IN BAKING TINS

Poppy Seed Cake

Pastry:
6 oz. (170 g) plain flour
a pinch of Oetker Baking Powder Backin
2½ oz. (70 g) sugar
1 packet Oetker Vanillin Sugar
3½ oz. (100 g) butter or margarine

Filling:
5½ oz. (150 g) poppy seeds
4 egg yolks
1 tbsp. warm water
5½ oz. (150 g) sugar
5 drops Oetker Baking Essence, lemon flavour
a pinch of salt
4 egg whites
1¾ oz. (50 g) Oetker Gustin (corn starch powder)
1 oz. (30 g) sultanas (washed and well drained)
1¾ oz. (50 g) candied lemon peel (diced)

For the pastry, mix and sieve together the flour and the Backin onto a pastry board or cool slab. Make a well in the centre and pour in the sugar and the vanillin sugar. Add the cold fat, cut into small pieces, cover the whole with flour and, starting from the middle, work all the ingredients quickly with the hands into a smooth, firm paste. If sticky, cool well through for some time.
Roll out ⅔ of the pastry to fit the base of a round cake tin with a removable rim (diameter about 10½ in.) (26 cm). Prick well with a fork and bake till golden.

Oven: pre-heat for 5 minutes at very hot, bake at very hot.

Baking time: 25–30 minutes.

Allow the pastry base to cool. Form the rest of the pastry to a long roll; lay this roll round the inside of the rim and press it against the sides so that it is 1½ in. (3 cm) high.

For the filling, grind the poppy seeds. Using a wire whisk, whisk the egg yolks until frothy; gradually add ⅔ of the sugar; continue whisking until the mixture is thick and creamy, add the flavourings. Whisk the egg whites until stiff, they must be so firm that a cut with a knife remains visible; add the rest of the sugar gradually, whisking all the time. Fill the whisked egg whites onto the egg yolk mixture, sieve the Gustin over it and add the poppy seeds, the currants and the candied peel. Fold all the ingredients carefully into the egg yolk mixture – do not stir. Fill into the baked pastry case and smooth the surface evenly.

Oven: moderately hot.

Baking time: 25–30 minutes.

Lemon-Chocolate Cake

Pastry:
11 oz. (300 g) plain flour
2 level tsp. (6 g) Oetker Baking Powder Backin
1 level tbsp. cocoa
6 oz. (170 g) sugar
1 packet Oetker Vanillin Sugar
1 egg
6 oz. (170 g) butter or margarine
7 oz. (200 g) ground hazelnuts

Icing:
1³/₄ oz. (50 g) milk chocolate
1 tbsp. coconut butter

Filling:
3 level tsp. Oetker Regina Gelatine, ground white
3 tbsp. cold water for soaking
5 lumps sugar
7 tbsp. lemon juice
1³/₄ pt. fresh double cream
5¹/₂ oz. (150 g) icing sugar

For the pastry, mix and sieve together the flour, Backin and cocoa onto a pastry board or cool slab. Make a well in the centre and pour in the sugar, vanillin sugar and egg. Draw in some of the flour from the sides of the well to mix with these to form a thick paste. Cut the cold fat into small pieces, add to the paste, cover with the hazelnuts and starting from the middle, knead all the ingredients quickly into a smooth paste. If it should stick cool well through for a time. Prepare four layers from the pastry by rolling out a quarter each time onto the greased base (without a raised edge) of a round cake tin, diameter about 10¹/₂ in. (26 cm) with removable rim. Bake with rim removed.

Oven: pre-heat for 5 minutes at very hot, bake at very hot.

Baking time: 10–15 minutes.

Remove each layer from the base immediately after baking and cut up one of the layers into 16 segments. Leave to cool.

For the icing break up the chocolate into small pieces and place, with the coconut butter, in a small saucepan. Heat very gently (a double saucepan may be used) until all can be well blended. Coat the 16 segments evenly on one side with the icing.

For the filling, mix the gelatine with the water and leave 10 minutes to swell. Rub the lemon skin with the corners of the sugar lumps. Heat the soaked gelatine with the sugar lumps, stirring all the time until all is dissolved; add the lemon juice and leave to cool. Whisk the cream until almost stiff, then add the lukewarm gelatine mixture gradually; finish whipping the cream then fold in the sieved icing sugar.

Fill some of the cream into a forcing bag. Divide one cake layer into 16 imaginary segments and pipe onto each segment a cone-shaped pattern of "lying down rings" close together, starting very small in the middle and increasing steadily in size to the outside edge. Coat the other two layers on one side with the rest of the cream (pipe on if desired). Sandwich the layers together placing the decorated layer on top. Take an iced segment and place on its side, point to the middle, leaning against the cream cone; continue thus with the remaining segments thus achieving a fan-like pattern.

Cool the cake well through until it is to be eaten.

Fruit Flan (Phot. page 90)

Pastry:
5½ oz. (150 g) plain flour
½ level tsp. (1½ g) Oetker Baking Powder Backin
2½ oz. (70 g) sugar
1 packet Oetker Vanillin Sugar
1 small egg
2½ oz. (70 g) butter or margarine
1 level tbsp. plain flour for the flan rim

Custard filling:
1 packet Oetker Sauce Powder, vanilla flavour
1 well heaped tbsp. sugar
¼ pt. (140 ccm) and 6 tbsp. cold milk
about 1½ lb. (680 g) raw, stewed, tinned or bottled (apples, apricots, strawberries, cherries, peaches, gooseberries, etc.)

Glaze:
1 packet Oetker Cake Glaze, transparent
almost ½ pt. (285 ccm) water or fruit juice
sugar according to the directions on the packet

Pastry quantity for a small flan:
1¾ oz. (50 g) plain flour
a pinch of Oetker Baking Powder Backin
1 slightly heaped tbsp. sugar
½ packet Oetker Vanillin Sugar
2 tbsp. milk
1 oz. (30 g) butter or margarine
1 level tsp. plain flour for the flan rim

Fruit topping:
about 9 oz. (250 g) fresh, stewed, or tinned fruit

For the pastry, mix and sieve together the flour and the Backin onto a pastry board or cool slab. Make a well in the centre and pour in the sugar, vanillin sugar and egg (or milk). Draw in some of the flour from the sides of the well to mix with these to form a thickish paste. Add the cold fat, cut into small pieces. Cover the whole with flour and starting from the middle, work all these ingredients quickly with the hands into a smooth firm paste. If it should be sticky cool well through for a while. Roll out ⅔ of the pastry to fit the base of a round cake tin with a removable rim*, 10½ in. (26 cm) in diameter, or a smaller tin of 6 in. (16 cm) diameter. Knead the flour into the rest of the pastry, form a long roll and lay this around the inside of the rim. Press it against the sides so that it is 1–1½ in. (2–3 cm) high. Prick well with a fork.

Oven: pre-heat for 5 minutes at very hot, bake at moderately hot.
Baking time: 15–20 minutes.

Continued on next page

*If a special flan tin is used (diameter 11 in. (28 cm)) roll out ⅔ of the pastry to a round shape of a good 11½ in. (29 cm) diameter and lay this on the tin (dust first with breadcrumbs). Form the rest of the pastry into a roll and lay this in the hollow within the circumference; press so that the surface is even. Prick well with a fork.

Glaze:
1/2 packet Oetker Cake Glaze, transparent
9 tbsp. water or fruit juice
2 slightly heaped tsp. sugar
  (if water is used)
or
1 slightly heaped tsp. sugar
  (if fruit juice is used)
For decorating:
a few almonds or hazelnuts (sliced)

For the custard filling (for the larger cake only), mix the sauce powder with the sugar and gradually blend in the milk. Bring to the boil, stirring all the time and allow to boil up briefly. Cool, stirring frequently, then spread evenly over the base of the flan shell.

For the fruit topping, use soft fruit such as apricots, strawberries and peaches uncooked, preparing it as follows: wash carefully, drain well and stone, or remove stalks. Stewed fruit (apples should be washed, peeled, and cut into quarters or eighths) should be carefully poached in syrup (sugar and water).
Bottled or tinned fruit should be well drained.
Place the prepared fruit on the flan shell.
Prepare the glaze according to the instructions on the packet and pour it over the fruit. Decorate the edge with sliced almonds or hazelnuts.

Linzer Cake

Pastry:
7 oz. (200 g) plain flour
1 level tsp. (3 g) Oetker Baking Powder Backin
4 1/2 oz. (125 g) sugar
1 packet Oetker Vanillin Sugar
2 drops Oetker Baking Essence, bitter almond flavour
a pinch of ground cloves
1 level tsp. ground cinnamon
1 egg white, 1/2 egg yolk
4 1/2 oz. (125 g) butter or margarine
4 1/2 oz. (125 g) ground almonds or hazelnuts
Filling:
about 3 1/2 oz. (100 g) jam
For brushing:
1/2 egg yolk and 1 tsp. milk

For the pastry, mix and sieve together the flour and the Backin onto a pastry board or cool slab. Make a well in the centre and pour in the sugar, vanillin sugar, spices, egg white and 1/2 egg yolk. Draw in some of the flour from the sides of the well and mix with these to form a thickish paste. Add the cold fat, cut into small pieces and the ground almonds or hazelnuts. Cover the whole with more of the flour and, starting from the middle, work all these ingredients quickly with the hands into a smooth firm paste. If it should be sticky cool well through for some time.
Roll out a little less than half the pastry to the same size as the base of a round cake tin with a removable rim, diameter 10 1/2 in. (26 cm) and then cut it into 16–20 equally narrow strips. Roll out the rest of the pastry to line the base of the round cake tin. Spread with the jam, leaving 1/2 in. free round the edge. Make a criss cross pattern over the jam with the strips of pastry and brush these with egg yolk and milk, beaten together.
Oven: moderately hot.
Baking time: 25–30 minutes.

Cottage Cheese Flan with Cream (Phot. page 53)

Pastry:
3½ oz. (100 g) plain flour
a pinch of Oetker Baking Powder Backin
1 well heaped tbsp. sugar
1 packet Oetker Vanillin Sugar
2½ oz. (70 g) butter or margarine

Flan filling:
2 packets Oetker Regina Gelatine, powdered, white
6 tbsp. cold water for blending
4½ oz. (125 g) butter or margarine
9 oz. (250 g) sugar
3 egg yolks
1⅛ lb. (500 g) cottage cheese
grated rind of half a lemon
juice of 1 lemon
3 egg whites
½ pt. (285 ccm) fresh double cream

For the pastry, mix and sieve together the flour and the Backin onto a pastry board or cool slab. Make a well in the centre and pour in the sugar and vanillin sugar. Add the cold fat, cut into small pieces. Cover the whole with flour and, starting from the middle, work all the ingredients quickly with the hands into a smooth firm paste. If it should be sticky, cool well through for some time.

Roll out the pastry to fit the base of a round cake tin with a removable rim of 10½ in. (26 cm) diameter. Prick well with a fork and bake.

Oven: pre-heat for 5 minutes at very hot, bake at moderately hot.

Baking time: about 15 minutes.

Loosen the pastry shell from the cake tin base after removing from the oven. When quite cold remove to a large flat plate and clip the rim of the cake tin round it again.

For the flan filling, blend the gelatine with water and leave ten minutes to swell. Then heat gently, stirring all the time until the gelatine is quite dissolved, then cool. Cream the fat and beat in gradually ⅔ of the sugar alternately with the egg yolks. Rub the cottage cheese through a fine sieve and add, together with the grated lemon rind, lemon juice and luke-warm gelatine liquid to the creamed ingredients. Mix well together. Whisk the egg whites till stiff; the snow must be so firm that a cut with the knife remains visible. Add gradually the rest of the sugar, whisking all the time. Whip the cream, then fold it and the egg whites into the cottage cheese mixture. Spread the filling evenly over the baked pastry base and smooth evenly. Cool the cake through well until the filling is firm, then loosen from the cake rim with a knife.

Alternatively cherries may be added to the filling. Use 1⅛ lb. (500 g) stoned cherries (stewed, bottled or tinned) and drain them well. Spread half of the cottage cheese cream filling onto the pastry base, distribute the cherries evenly over it, leaving ½ in. (1 cm) free round the edge and spread the rest of the filling over the cherries, smoothing evenly.

This cake may be decorated attractively with candied fruits, cut into pieces, e.g. pineapples, cherries or candied peel.

Apple or Cherry Tart

Pastry:
11 oz. (310 g) plain flour
2 level tsp. (6 g) Oetker Baking Powder Backin
3½ oz. (100 g) sugar
1 packet Oetker Vanillin Sugar
a pinch of salt
½ egg yolk
1 egg white
1 tbsp. milk
5½ oz. (150 g) butter or margarine

Apple filling:
2¼–3¼ lbs. (1–1½ kg) apples
1 tbsp. water
2–3 well heaped tbsp. sugar
½ tsp. ground cinnamon
1¾ oz. (50 g) sultanas (washed and well drained)
a few drops of Oetker rum flavour
or Oetker Baking Essence, lemon flavour

or

Cherry filling:
2¼ lbs. (1 kg) Morello cherries
3½–4½ oz. (100–125 g) sugar
a few drops Oetker Baking Essence, lemon flavour
3 slightly heaped tbsp. Oetker Gustin (corn starch powder)

For brushing:
½ egg yolk and 1 tbsp. milk

For the pastry, mix and sieve together the flour and the Backin onto a pastry board or cool slab. Make a well in the centre and pour in the sugar, vanillin sugar, salt, ½ egg yolk, egg white and the milk. Draw in some of the flour from the sides of the well and mix with these to form a thickish paste. Add the cold fat, cut into small pieces. Cover the whole with more of the flour and, starting from the middle, work all these ingredients quickly with the hands into a smooth, firm paste. If it should be sticky, cool well through for some time. Grease a round cake tin of 10½ in. (26 cm) diameter with a removable rim. Roll out about half of the pastry to fit the base and prick well with a fork.

Oven: moderately hot.

Baking time: 20–30 minutes.

For the apple filling, peel and core the apples. Slice them and stew over a low heat, together with the water, cinnamon and sultanas. Stir frequently until the apples are cooked, then set aside to cool. Add sugar to taste and the flavouring.

For the cherry filling, wash and stone the cherries, sprinkle with sugar and leave to stand for a while. Bring to the boil, remove from heat and drain the cherries in a sieve or colander, catching the juice below. When both juice and cherries are cold, measure off ½ pt. (285 ccm) of the juice (if necessary add water) and season with the flavourings. Blend 4 tbsp. juice with the Gustin. Bring the rest to the boil, remove from heat, stir in the prepared Gustin and bring to the boil again briefly. Add the cherries and cool again.

From the rest of the pastry roll out another layer the size of the cake base, then make a long finger-thick roll. Lay this on the precooked cake base around the inside of the rim. Press, sealing well to the cooked base and against the sides of the tin so that it is about 1¼ in. (3 cm) high.

Fill the cold fruit mass into the case and lay the uncooked pastry layer on the top. Beat the egg yolk with the milk and brush over the cake. Prick well with a fork.

Oven: pre-heat for 5 minutes at very hot, bake at moderately hot.

Baking time: 15–20 minutes.

Fruit Crumble Cake

Pastry:
5½ oz. (150 g) plain flour
½ level tsp. (1½ g) Oetker Baking Powder Backin
2½ oz. (70 g) sugar
1 packet Oetker Vanillin Sugar
1 small egg
2½ oz. (70 g) butter or margarine
1 tbsp. plain flour for the flan rim

Fruit filling:
about 1½ lbs. (680 g) apples or plums

Crumble topping:
5½ oz. (150 g) plain flour
2½–3½ oz. (70–100 g) sugar
1 packet Oetker Vanillin Sugar
a pinch of ground cinnamon
2½–3½ oz. (70–100 g) butter or margarine

If the crumbly mixture should become too fine, add a few drops of milk; if the lumps are too large, add more flour.

For the pastry, mix and sieve together the flour and Backin onto a pastry board or cool slab. Make a well in the centre and pour in the sugar, vanillin sugar and egg. Draw in some of the flour from the sides of the well to mix with these to form a thickish paste. Add the cold fat, cut into small pieces, and cover the whole with more of the flour. Starting from the middle, work all these ingredients quickly with the hands into a smooth firm paste. If sticky, cool well through.
Roll out ⅔ of the pastry to cover the base of a round cake tin with a removable rim 10½ in. (26 cm) diameter. Knead the tablespoon of flour into the rest of the pastry, form a long roll and lay it round the inside of the rim. Press it against the sides so that it is 1–1½ in. (2–3 cm) high. Prick well with a fork.
Oven: pre-heat for 5 minutes at very hot, bake at moderately hot.
Baking time: 15–20 minutes.
For the filling, peel and core the apples and cut into small pieces. Wash and stone the plums and cut into quarters. Spread the apple or plum filling evenly over the cooled pastry case.
For the crumble topping, sieve the flour into a bowl and mix in the sugar, vanillin sugar and cinnamon. Flake the cold fat into the dry ingredients and mix the whole into a crumbly mass with two forks. Distribute the crumble topping over the fruit in the pastry case.
Oven: moderately hot.
Baking time: 25–30 minutes.

Cottage Cheese White Bread

Dough:
1¾ oz. (50 g) butter or margarine
2 well heaped tbsp. sugar
a pinch of salt
9 oz. (250 g) cottage cheese rubbed through a fine sieve
1⅛ lb. (500 g) plain flour
2 packets Oetker Baking Powder Backin
7 tbsp. milk or milk and whey

For brushing:
a little milk

Cream the fat and gradually add the sugar, salt and cottage cheese. Mix and sieve together the flour and Backin and add ⅔ of it alternately with the liquid. Empty the rest of the flour onto a pastry board or cool slab and tip the soft mixture onto it. Knead the rest of the flour into the mixture so that the dough becomes firm. (This may be a little difficult in the final stages, but do not add more liquid.) Grease a loaf baking tin and place the dough in it, making a cut down the middle lengthways of ½ in. (1 cm) deep. Brush with milk.
Oven: moderately hot.
Baking time: 45–60 minutes.

Cottage Cheese Cake

Pastry:
5½ oz. (150 g) plain flour
1 level tsp. (3 g) Oetker Baking Powder Backin
2½ oz. (70 g) sugar
2 egg yolks
1 tbsp. milk or water
1¾ oz. (50 g) butter or margarine
1 level tbsp. plain flour for the flan rim

Filling:
2 packets Oetker Pudding Powder, vanilla flavour
1 heaped tsp. Oetker Gustin (corn starch powder)
7 oz. (200 g) sugar
1 pt. (570 ccm) cold milk
½ bottle Oetker Baking Essence, lemon flavour
1 lb. 10 oz. (740 g) cottage cheese
3 egg whites

For brushing:
1 egg yolk and 1 tbsp. milk

For the pastry, mix and sieve together the flour and the Backin onto a pastry board or cool slab. Make a well in the centre and pour in the sugar, egg yolks and liquid. Draw in some of the flour from the sides of the well to mix with these to form a thickish paste. Add the cold fat, cut into small pieces, cover the whole with more of the flour and, starting from the middle, work all these ingredients quickly with the hands into a smooth firm paste. Roll out ⅔ of the pastry to fit the base of a round cake tin with a removable rim, diameter 10½ in. (26 cm), Knead the tbsp. of flour into the rest of the pastry; form it into a long roll and lay this around the inside of the rim. Press it against the sides so that it is 1½ in. (3 cm) high. Prick well with a fork.

Oven: pre-heat for 5 minutes at very hot, bake at moderately hot.
Baking time: about 15 minutes.

For the filling, blend the pudding powder and ⅔ of the sugar with ½ pt. (285 ccm) milk. Heat the rest of the milk, and when it boils remove from heat and stir in the pudding powder mixture. Return to heat and allow to boil up once more. Remove from heat and add the lemon flavouring. Rub the cottage cheese through a fine sieve and add to the mixture. Allow to boil up once more, stirring all the time. Empty the hot mass into a mixing bowl. Whisk the egg whites until stiff and fold in the rest of the sugar. Fold this egg white snow into the cottage cheese mixture. Fill into the baked pastry shell and smooth evenly. Beat the egg yolk with the milk and brush carefully over the surface of the cottage cheese filling.

Oven: slow.
Baking time: 45–60 minutes.

The filling should scarcely rise at all during baking, otherwise it may collapse afterwards. If necessary turn down the heat. After baking loosen the cake from the sides of the tin with a knife but allow to cool in the tin. Before weighing the cottage cheese, remove the whey by pressing it through a cloth. If the cheese is very moist, it may be necessary to buy double the amount.

CAKES ON A BAKING SHEET

Filled Mocca Biscuits

Pastry:
(sufficient for 20 filled biscuits)
9 oz. (250 g) plain flour
5 slightly heaped tbsp. Oetker Gustin (corn starch powder)
2 level tbsp. cocoa
1 level tsp. (3 g) Oetker Baking Powder Backin
2½ oz. (70 g) sugar
1 egg
1 tbsp. milk or water
5½ oz. (150 g) butter or margarine

Icing:
3½ oz. (100 g) icing sugar
2 level tbsp. cocoa
1–2 tbsp. hot water
1 oz. (30 g) melted butter or margarine

For decorating:
a few almonds (blanched and chopped)

Mocca filling:
½ packet Oetker Pudding Powder, vanilla flavour
1 slightly heaped tsp. Oetker Gustin (corn starch powder)
2 well heaped tbsp. sugar
½ pt. (285 ccm) cold milk
3½ oz. (100 g) butter or margarine
1 well heaped tsp. instant coffee powder

For the pastry, mix and sieve together the flour, Gustin, cocoa and Backin onto a pastry board or cool slab. Make a well in the centre and pour in the sugar, egg and liquid. Draw in some of the flour from the sides of the well to mix with these ingredients to form a thickish paste. Add the cold fat, cut into small pieces, and cover the whole with more of the flour. Starting from the middle, work all these ingredients quickly with the hands into a smooth firm paste. If it should be sticky, cool well through for a while.
Roll out the pastry thinly and cut out round shapes, 3¼ in. (8 cm) in diameter. Lay them on a baking sheet.

Oven: pre-heat for 5 minutes at very hot, bake at moderately hot.

Baking time: 10–15 minutes.

For the icing, sieve together the icing sugar and cocoa and blend with as much water as will give a thick coating consistency. Add the hot fat. Coat half the biscuits on the top surface with the icing and decorate round the edge with the chopped almonds.

For the filling, blend the pudding powder and the sugar with 3 tbsp. of the milk. Bring the rest of the milk to the boil, remove from heat, stir in the prepared pudding mixture and bring to the boil again briefly. Then stir in the instant coffee powder very carefully and leave to cool. Stir now and again to prevent a skin forming.
Cream the fat and beat in the cold pudding, a tablespoon at a time (neither the fat nor the pudding should be too cold otherwise the mixture may curdle).
Pipe the mocca filling in a spiral pattern on the underside of the biscuits which have not been iced and lay an iced biscuit on top of each.

Fruit or Cottage Cheese Cake

Pastry:
13 oz. (370 g) plain flour
4 level tsp. (12 g) Oetker Baking Powder Backin
2½ oz. (70 g) sugar
1 packet Oetker Vanillin Sugar
1 egg white
½ egg yolk
5 tbsp. milk or water
5½ oz. (150 g) butter or margarine

Apple filling:
3½ lb. (1½ kg) apples
1¾–4½ oz. (50–125 g) sugar
1¾ oz. (50 g) currants or sultanas (washed and well drained)
a few drops Oetker rum flavour

or

Cherry filling:
3½ lb. (1½ kg) Morello cherries
6 oz. (175 g) sugar
5 slightly heaped tbsp. Oetker Gustin (corn starch powder)

or

1 packet Oetker Pudding Powder, vanilla flavour

or

Cottage cheese filling:
2¼ lb. (1 kg) cottage cheese (well pressed out)
1 packet Oetker Sauce Powder, vanilla flavour

or

½ packet Oetker Pudding Powder, vanilla flavour
1 egg
7–9 oz. (200–250 g) sugar
5 drops Oetker Baking Essence, lemon flavour
1¾ oz. (50 g) sultanas (washed and well drained)

For brushing:
½ egg yolk and 1 tbsp. milk

For the pastry, mix and sieve together the flour and Backin onto a pastry board or cool slab. Make a well in the centre and pour in the sugar, vanillin sugar, egg white, the ½ egg yolk and liquid. Draw in some of the flour from the sides of the well to mix with these ingredients to form a thickish paste. Add the cold fat, cut into small pieces, and cover the whole with more of the flour. Starting from the middle, work all these ingredients quickly with the hands into a firm smooth paste. If it should be sticky, add some flour. Roll out almost half of the pastry into a shape the size of the baking sheet. Place a large sheet of paper on top and roll pastry and paper carefully up together. Lay aside. Grease a baking sheet. Roll out the rest of the pastry into a sheet a little larger than the baking sheet. Roll it loosely on the rolling pin then unroll onto the baking sheet.

For the apple filling, wash, peel and core the apples and slice them. Stew, together with the sultanas and 2 tbsp. sugar, over a slow heat until cooked, stirring frequently. Cool slightly and flavour to taste with the rest of the sugar and the lemon flavour.

For the cherry filling, wash and stone the cherries, sprinkle with sugar and leave to stand for a while. Bring to the boil, remove from heat and drain the cherries in a sieve or colander, catching the juice below. When both juice and cherries are cold, measure off ½ pt. (285 ccm) of the juice (if necessary make up the amount with water). Blend the Gustin or the pudding powder with 4 tbsp. of the juice and bring the rest to the boil. Remove from heat, stir in the prepared Gustin or pudding powder mixture and boil up once more. Stir in the well-drained cherries and cool well through.

For the cottage cheese filling, rub the cottage cheese through a fine sieve. Add the sauce or pudding powder, egg, sugar, lemon flavour and sultanas and mix all well together. Spread the filling over the pastry on the baking sheet, leaving about 1 in free (2 cm) on the open side of the baking sheet. Beat the egg yolk and the milk. Fold the edges of the pastry over the filling and brush with the egg yolk and milk. Carefully unroll the pastry top from the paper onto the filling and brush with the beaten egg and milk. Prick well with a fork.

Oven: pre-heat for 5 minutes at very hot, bake at moderately hot. **Baking time:** 20–30 minutes.

Apple or Cherry Roll

Pastry:
10½ oz. (300 g) plain flour
1 packet Oetker Baking Powder Backin
2½ oz. (70 g) sugar
1 packet Oetker Vanillin Sugar
3 drops Oetker Baking Essence, bitter almond flavour
a pinch of salt
1 egg
3½ oz. (100 g) butter or margarine
4½ oz. (125 g) cottage cheese (well pressed out)

Apple filling:
2¼–3½ lb. (1–1½ kg) apples
2½ oz. (70 g) sugar
1¾ oz. (50 g) sultanas (washed and well drained)
3–4 drops Oetker Baking Essence, lemon flavour

or

Cherry filling:
2¼–3½ lb. (1–1½ kg) morello cherries
4½ oz. (125 g) sugar
1¾ oz. (50 g) Oetker Gustin (corn starch powder)

For brushing:
some sugared milk

For sprinkling:
coarse-grained sugar

For the pastry, mix and sieve together the flour and Backin onto a pastry board or cool slab. Make a well in the centre and pour in the sugar, vanillin sugar, baking essence, salt and egg. Draw in some of the flour from the sides of the well and mix with these to form a thickish paste. Add the cold fat, cut into small pieces, and the cottage cheese (if preferred, rubbed through a fine sieve). Cover all with more of the flour and, starting from the middle, work all these ingredients quickly with the hands into a smooth firm paste. If it should stick, add more flour.

For the apple filling, peel and core the apples and slice them. Cook them over a slow heat, together with the sugar and sultanas and stirring all the time until the apples are done. Flavour to taste with the baking essence and leave to cool.

For the cherry filling, wash and stone the cherries, sprinkle with the sugar and leave to stand for some time. Bring them to the boil, remove from heat and drain in a sieve or colander, catching the juice below. When both, juice and cherries are cold, measure off ½ pt. (285 ccm) (make up the amount with water if necessary). Blend the Gustin with 4 tbsp. of the juice and bring the rest to the boil. Remove from heat, stir in the prepared Gustin and boil up again briefly. Stir in the cherries and leave to cool.

Divide the pastry into two halves and roll out each piece to a oblong shape 20×12 in. (40×30 cm). Pile half of the fruit filling on an area 1.6 in. (4 cm) of the width and the whole of the length, leaving a good 2 in. (5 cm) free at the sides. Fold these sides over the filling and roll up like a swiss roll. Press the ends firmly together and flatten the rolls a little. Brush over with the milk and sprinkle with the sugar. Using a sharp knife, make parallel cuts in the rolls ¼ in. (½ cm) deep and 1½ in. (3 cm) apart. Grease a baking sheet and lay the rolls on it.

Oven: moderately hot.
Baking time: 25–30 minutes.
When cold cut the rolls into even slices of 1 in. (2½ cm).

Cottage Cheese Cream Cake   Recipe page 111
Cottage Cheese Flan with Cream   Recipe page 46

Strudel Pastry

7 oz. (200 g) plain flour
a pinch of salt
5 tbsp. luke-warm water
1³/₄ oz. (50 g) butter or margarine
 or lard (melted)
 or 3 tbsp. oil

Sieve the flour onto a pastry board or cool slab. Make a well in the centre. Put into it the salt. Pour in the water and fat slowly, at the same time drawing flour from the sides of the well to form a thickish paste. Cover the whole with more flour and starting from the middle, knead the whole to a smooth firm paste. Lay the strudel pastry on some greaseproof paper in a hot, dry enamel saucepan (boil water in it beforehand). Shut the pan with a lid and leave the pastry to rest for half an hour. The following cakes are prepared with this pastry:

Viennese Apple Strudel

Strudel pastry quantity and method see above
For brushing:
2¹/₂ oz. (70 g) butter or margarine
 (melted)
Apple filling:
2¹/₄–3¹/₂ lb. (1–1¹/₂ kg) apples
1 bottle Oetker rum flavour
3 drops Oetker Baking Essence,
 lemon flavour
1³/₄ oz. (50 g) breadcrumbs
3¹/₂ oz. (100 g) sugar
1 packet Oetker Vanillin Sugar
1³/₄ oz. (50 g) sultanas
 (washed and well drained)
1³/₄ oz. (50 g) almonds
 (blanched and chopped)

For the filling, wash, peel and slice the apples finely. Mix them with the lemon and rum flavourings.
Roll out the strudel pastry on a large, white, floured cloth (e.g. a tablecloth). Brush thinly with some of the fat and then pull out with the hands until it is about 20 × 18 in. (50 × 70 cm). It must become transparent. If the edges are thicker than the rest, cut them off. Brush the pastry over with a good ²/₃ of the fat. Distribute the breadcrumbs over ²/₃ of the pastry, starting from the longer side of the rectangle and leaving 1¹/₂ in. (3 cm) free along the shorter sides. Distribute the apples over the area covered with breadcrumbs and sprinkle over them the sugar, vanillin sugar, sultanas and almonds. Fold over the apples the 1¹/₂ in. (3 cm) border at the sides that was left free of filling and, starting from the long side covered with filling, roll up like a swiss roll. Press the ends well, lay the roll on a well greased baking sheet and brush again with the fat.

Oven: pre-heat for 5 minutes at very hot,
 bake at moderately hot.

Baking time: 45–55 minutes.

The crust will be improved if the strudel is brushed over with the remaining fat during baking.
Instead of one large roll, two smaller ones may be made and baked side by side on a baking sheet.

Tea Biscuits   Recipe page 64

Viennese Poppy Seed Strudel

Strudel pastry quantity and method see page 57

For brushing:
1³/₄ oz. (50 g) butter or margarine (melted)

Filling:
9 oz. (250 g) poppy seeds
4¹/₂ oz. (125 g) sugar
1 packet Oetker Vanillin Sugar
4 drops Oetker Baking Essence, lemon flavour
¹/₂ level tsp. ground cinnamon
1³/₄ oz. (50 g) butter or margarine (melted)
a little less than ¹/₂ pt. (285 ccm) hot milk
1³/₄ oz. (50 g) sultanas (washed and well drained)

For the filling, grind the poppy seeds and mix with the sugar and flavourings. Stir in the fat and as much of the milk as will give a mixture which can be spread although it should not be soft. Set aside to cool.

Roll out the strudel pastry on a large white floured cloth (e.g. a tablecloth). Brush thinly with some of the fat and then pull with the hands until it is about 20 × 28 in. (50 × 70 cm). It must become transparent. If the edges are thicker then the pastry, cut them off. Brush the pastry with a little more than ¹/₂ the remaining fat and distribute the poppy seed filling over ²/₃ of the pastry starting from the longer side and leaving 1¹/₂ in. (3 cm) free along the edges of the shorter sides. Sprinkle the sultanas over the filling. Fold the free edges at the sides over the filling and starting at the long side, roll up like a swiss roll. Press the ends well, lay the roll on a greased baking sheet and brush again with the fat.

Oven: pre-heat for 5 minutes at very hot, bake at moderately hot.
Baking time: 45–55 minutes.

The crust will be improved if the strudel is brushed over with the remaining fat during baking.
Instead of one large roll, two smaller ones may be made and baked, side by side on the baking sheet.

Fruit Tartlets (Phot. page 90)

Pastry:
(sufficient for 12–14 tartlets of 4 in. (10 cm) diameter)
7 oz. (200 g) plain flour
1 level tsp. (3 g) Oetker Baking Powder Backin
2¹/₂ oz. (70 g) sugar
1 packet Oetker Vanillin Sugar
a pinch of salt
4 drops Oetker Baking Essence, lemon flavour
2 tbsp. water
3¹/₂ oz. (100 g) butter or margarine

For the pastry, mix and sieve together the flour and Backin onto a pastry board or cool slab. Make a well in the centre and pour in the sugar, vanillin sugar, baking essence, salt and water. Draw in some of the flour from the sides of the well and mix with these ingredients to form a thickish paste. Add the cold fat, cut into small pieces, and cover the whole with more of the flour. Starting from the middle, work all these ingredients quickly with the hands into a firm smooth paste. If it should stick, cool well through for some time.

Roll out the pastry 0.12 in. (3 mm) thick and cut out round shapes 4 in. (10 cm) in diameter. Lay them on a baking sheet and prick well with a fork.

Oven: pre-heat for 5 minutes at very hot, bake at moderately hot.
Baking time: 10–15 minutes.

Continued on next page

Filling:
1 packet Oetker Sauce Powder, vanilla flavour
1 well heaped tbsp. sugar
1/4 pt. (140 ccm) and 6 tbsp. cold milk
about 1 1/2 lb. (680 g) raw, stewed, tinned or bottled fruit (apples, apricots, strawberries, cherries, peaches, gooseberries, etc.)

Glaze:
1 packet Oetker Cake Glaze transparent, almost 1/2 pt. (285 ccm) water or fruit juice
sugar according to the directions of the packet

For decorating:
1/5–1/2 pt. (115–285 ccm) fresh double cream
sugar to taste

For the filling, mix together the sauce powder and the sugar and gradually blend in the milk. Bring to the boil, stirring all the time and boil briefly. Leave to cool, stirring all the time to prevent a skin forming. Spread evenly on the baked pastry rounds.

Fresh fruit should be prepared as follows: wash apricots, strawberries, blueberries and peaches. Drain well and pick over or remove stones and stems according to kind. Stewed, bottled or tinned fruit should be well drained. Arrange the prepared fruit on the pastry rounds, leaving about 1/2 in. (1 cm) round the edge.

Prepare the glaze according to the instructions on the packet and spoon it over the fruit.

Whip the cream and sweeten to taste. Pipe around the edges of the tartlets.

Hazelnut Ring

Pastry:
10 1/2 oz. (300 g) plain flour
2 level tsp. (3 g) Oetker Baking Powder Backin
3 1/2 oz. (100 g) sugar
1 packet Oetker Vanillin Sugar
1 egg
2 tbsp. milk or water
4 1/2 oz. (125 g) butter or margarine

Filling:
7 oz. (200 g) ground hazelnuts
3 1/2 oz. (100 g) sugar
4–5 drops Oetker Baking Essence, bitter almond flavour
1/2 egg yolk
1 egg white
3–4 tbsp. water

For brushing:
1/2 egg yolk and 1 tbsp. milk

For the pastry, mix and sieve together the flour and the Backin onto a pastry board or cool slab. Make a well in the centre and pour in the sugar, vanillin sugar, egg and liquid. Draw in some of the flour from the sides of the well to mix with these ingredients to form a thickish paste. Add the cold fat, cut into small pieces, and cover the whole with more of the flour. Starting from the middle, work all these ingredients quickly with the hands into a smooth firm paste. If it should be sticky, cool well through for a while. Roll out the pastry into a rectangle 14 in. by 18 in. (35 × 45 cm).

For the filling, mix the hazelnuts, sugar, baking essence, the half egg yolk and the egg white with as much of the water as will give a mixture which can be spread. Spread this filling on the pastry and roll up, like a swiss roll, starting at a long side.

Grease a baking sheet and lay the roll in the form of a ring on it. Beat the 1/2 egg yolk with the milk and brush over the ring. Make regular cuts of about 1/4 in. (1/2 cm) deep in the surface to give a star pattern.

Oven: moderately hot.
Baking time: about 45 minutes.
Alternatively 6 tbsp. of honey may be added to the filling.

Nut or Coconut Corners (Phot. page 145)

Pastry:
5½ oz. (150 g) plain flour
½ level tsp. Oetker Baking Powder Backin
2½ oz. (70 g) sugar
1 packet Oetker Vanillin Sugar
1 egg
2½ oz. (70 g) butter or margarine

Topping:
2 tbsp. apricot jam
3½ oz. (100 g) butter or margarine
3½ oz. (100 g) sugar
1 packet Oetker Vanillin Sugar
2 tbsp. water
7 oz. (200 g) hazelnuts (half ground, half chopped)
or
7 oz. (200 g) desiccated coconut

Icing:
2 well heaped tbsp. icing sugar
2 heaped tsp. cocoa
about 2 tbsp. hot water
a knob of butter or margarine (melted)

For the pastry, mix and sieve together the flour and Backin onto a pastry board or cool slab. Make a well in the centre and pour in the sugar, vanillin sugar and egg. Draw in some of the flour from the sides of the well and mix with these ingredients to form a thickish paste. Add the cold fat, cut into small pieces, and cover the whole with more of the flour. Starting from the middle, work all these ingredients quickly with the hands into a firm smooth paste. If it should stick, cool well through for some time.

Roll out the pastry into a rectangle 12 × 8 in. (32 × 24 cm). Lay this on the baking sheet and brush with the jam.

For the topping, melt the fat, sugar and vanillin sugar in a saucepan; add the water and boil up once. Stir in the hazelnuts or the desiccated coconut and leave to cool. Spread the topping over the jam on the pastry and lay a folded piece of paper at the open side.

Oven: moderately hot.

Baking time: 20–30 minutes.

Cool a little after baking, then cut into squares about 3¼ in. (8 cm). Cut these squares in half to give triangles.

For the icing, sieve together the cocoa and the icing sugar and blend with as much of the water as will give a thick coating consistency. Add the hot fat and brush over the two sharp corners of each triangle.

Filled Flana Biscuits

Pastry:
(sufficient for 20 filled biscuits)
9 oz. (250 g) plain flour
5 slightly heaped tbsp. Oetker Gustin (corn starch powder)
1 level tbsp. (3 g) Oetker Baking Powder Backin
2 well heaped tbsp. sugar
1 packet Oetker Vanillin Sugar
2 tbsp. sour cream or milk
6 oz. (170 g) butter or margarine

For the pastry, mix and sieve together the flour, Gustin and Backin onto a pastry board or cool slab. Make a well in the centre and pour in the sugar, vanillin sugar and cream or milk. Draw in some flour from the sides of the well to mix with these ingredients to form a thickish paste. Add the cold fat, cut into small pieces, and cover the whole with more of the flour. Starting from the middle, work all these ingredients quickly with the hands into a firm, smooth paste. If it should stick, cool well through for some time.

Roll out the pastry about 0.12 in. (3 mm) thick and with a pastry cutter cut out about 40 round shapes of 3¼ in. (7½ cm) diameter. Lay them on a baking sheet.

Oven: pre-heat for 5 minutes at very hot, bake at moderately hot.

Baking time: 12–15 minutes.

Continued on next page

Butter cream filling:
1 packet Oetker Chocolate Flana
2 well heaped tbsp. sugar
4 tbsp. cold milk for blending
½ pt. (285 ccm) milk
5½ oz. (150 g) butter or margarine
1 oz. (30 g) coconut butter (melted)
Icing:
2½ oz. (70 g) icing sugar
2 level tbsp. cocoa
1½ tbsp. hot water
1 oz. (30 g) melted coconut butter

For the butter cream filling, mix the contents of the Flana packet and the sugar well together in a cup. Add 2 tbsp. milk and beat well with a fork until no lumps can be seen. Mix in the other 2 tbsp. milk. Bring the ½ pt. milk to the boil, remove from heat, stir in the prepared Flana mixture slowly and boil up again for 1 minute, stirring all the time. Set aside to cool, stirring now and again to prevent a skin forming.

For the icing, sieve together the cocoa and icing sugar and blend with as much of the water as will give a thick coating consistency. Ice the tops of one half of the biscuits. Cream the fat and add the cold Flana, a tablespoon at a time (neither the fat nor the Flana should be too cold otherwise the mixture may curdle). Stir in the hot fat. Pipe the butter cream filling in a spiral on the underside of the biscuits which were not iced. Lay an iced one on top and decorate with a piped buttercream star in the middle.

Iced Rum Biscuits

Pastry:
10½ oz. (300 g) plain flour
2 level tsp. Oetker Baking Powder Backin
3½ oz. (100 g) sugar
1 packet Oetker Vanillin Sugar
1 egg
5½ oz. (150 g) butter or margarine
Filling:
a little jam
Icing:
4½ oz. (125 g) icing sugar
1 bottle Oetker rum flavour
1–1½ tbsp. hot water
For decorating:
candied cherries

For the pastry, mix and sieve together the flour and the Backin onto a pastry board or cool slab. Make a well in the centre and pour in the sugar, the vanillin sugar and the egg. Draw in some of the flour from the sides of the well to mix with these ingredients to form a thickish paste. Add the cold fat, cut into small pieces and cover the whole with more of the flour. Starting from the middle, work all these ingredients quickly with the hands into a smooth firm paste. If it should be sticky cool well through for some time.
Roll out the pastry thinly and cut out round shapes 3 in. (6 cm) in diameter. Lay them on a baking sheet.
Oven: pre-heat for 5 minutes at very hot,
bake at moderately hot.
Baking time: 8–12 minutes.
After the biscuits have cooled, spread the underside of one with jam and stick the underside of another against it. Pair off all the biscuits thus.
For the icing, blend the sieved icing sugar with the rum flavour and as much water as will give a thick coating consistency. Coat the top of each biscuit pair with the rum icing and decorate with half a candied cherry in the middle.

Terrace Biscuits

Pastry:
10½ oz. (300 g) plain flour
2 level tbsp. (6 g) Oetker Baking Powder Backin
3½ oz. (100 g) sugar
1 packet Oetker Vanillin Sugar
1 egg
5½ oz. (150 g) butter or margarine
Filling:
a little jam
For dusting:
a little icing sugar
For decorating:
a little red jam

For the pastry, mix and sieve the flour and the Backin onto a pastry board or cool slab. Make a well in the centre and pour in the sugar, vanillin sugar and egg. Draw in some of the flour from the sides of the well and mix with these to form a thickish paste. Add the cold fat, cut into small pieces and cover the whole with more of the flour. Starting from the middle, work all these ingredients quickly with the hands into a firm smooth paste. If it should stick, cool well through for some time. Roll out the pastry thinly and cut out biscuits of the same shape but in three different sizes (the same number of each size). Lay them on a baking sheet and bake till golden.
Oven: pre-heat for 5 minutes at very hot,
bake at moderately hot.
Baking time: 8–10 minutes.
Sort the biscuits into threes, one small, one middlesized and one large. Brush the underside of the 2 smaller ones with jam and stick the three together, the largest at the bottom then the middlesized one, then the smallest. Dust with icing sugar and decorate with a spot of jam.

Prassel Cake

Pastry:
13 oz. (375 g) plain flour
2 level tsp. (3 g) Oetker Baking Powder Backin
4½ oz. (125 g) sugar
1 bottle Oetker rum flavour
a pinch of salt
1 egg
7 oz. (200 g) butter or margarine
Jam and crumble topping:
7 oz. (200 g) apricot jam
12 oz. (340 g) plain flour
6 oz. (170 g) sugar
1 packet Oetker Vanillin Sugar
a pinch of ground cinnamon
6–7 oz. (170–200 g) butter or margarine
possibly 1–2 tbsp. water

For the pastry, mix and sieve together the flour and the Backin onto a pastry board or cool slab. Make a well in the centre and pour in the sugar, flavouring, salt and egg. Draw in some of the flour from the sides of the well to mix with these to form a thickish paste. Add the cold fat, cut into small pieces, and cover the whole with more of the flour. Starting from the middle, work all these ingredients quickly with the hands into a smooth firm paste. If it should be sticky, cool well through for some time.
Grease a baking sheet and roll out the pastry to cover it. Brush evenly with the jam.
For the crumble topping, sieve the flour into a bowl and mix with the sugar, vanillin sugar and cinnamon. Flake the cold fat into the dry ingredients and mix the whole into a crumble mass with two forks. If the mass does not crumble easily, add the 1–2 tbsp. water. Distribute the crumble topping over the jam on the pastry.
Oven: pre-heat for 5 minutes at very hot,
bake at moderately hot.
Baking time: about 25 minutes.

SMALL CAKES

Nut Ducats

Pastry:
13 oz. (370 g) plain flour
4¹/₂ oz. (125 g) Oetker Gustin
   (corn starch powder)
2 level tsp. (6 g) Oetker Baking
   Powder Backin
9 oz. (250 g) sugar
1 packet Oetker Vanillin Sugar
3 drops Oetker Baking Essence,
   bitter almond flavour
2 eggs
9 oz. (250 g) butter or margarine
9 oz. (250 g) hazelnuts (quartered)

Mix together the flour, Gustin and Backin and sieve onto a pastry board or cool slab. Make a well in the centre and pour in the sugar, vanillin sugar, baking essence and eggs. Draw in some of the flour from the sides of the well to mix with these ingredients to form a thickish paste. Add the cold fat, cut into small pieces, and the hazelnuts and cover the whole with more of the flour. Starting from the middle, work all these ingredients quickly with the hands into a firm smooth paste. Shape the pastry into several rolls about 1¹/₄ in. (2¹/₂ cm) thick, and leave in a cool place to stiffen. Then, using a sharp knife, cut off slices about ¹/₄ in. (¹/₂ cm) thick. Place on a baking sheet.

Oven: pre-heat for 5 minutes at very hot,
   bake at moderately hot.

Baking time: 10–15 minutes.

Almond Cookies

Pastry:
9 oz. (250 g) plain flour
1 level tsp. (3 g) Oetker Baking
   Powder Backin
3¹/₂ oz. (100 g) sugar
1 packet Oetker Vanillin Sugar
a pinch of salt
7 drops Oetker Baking Essence,
   bitter almond flavour
1 tbsp. milk
7 oz. (200 g) butter or margarine
For decorating:
2¹/₂ oz. (70 g) almonds (blanched)

Mix the flour with the Backin and sieve onto a pastry board or cool slab. Make a well in the centre and pour in the sugar, vanillin sugar, baking essence, salt and milk. Draw in some of the flour from the sides of the well to mix with these to form a thickish paste. Add the cold fat, cut into small pieces, and cover the whole with more of the flour. Starting from the middle, work all these ingredients quickly with the hands into a smooth firm paste. Form the pastry into 4 rolls about 1 in. (2 cm) thick, then flatten slightly with the ball of the hands until they are about 1¹/₂ in. (3 cm) in width and ¹/₂ in. (1 cm) high. Cool well through until they are stiff. Slice the strips into triangles, press an almond into each and place on a baking sheet.

Oven: pre-heat for 5 minutes at very hot,
   bake at moderately hot.

Baking time: 10–20 minutes.

Crunchies

Pastry:
10½ oz. (300 g) plain flour
2 level tsp. (6 g) Oetker Baking Powder Backin
3½–5½ oz. (100–150 g) sugar
1 packet Oetker Vanillin Sugar
1 bottle Oetker rum flavour
4 tbsp. milk
1¾ oz. (50 g) butter or margarine
1¾ oz. (50 g) lard
For brushing:
a little evaporated milk
For sprinkling:
a little sugar

Mix the flour and Backin and sieve onto a pastry board or cool slab. Make a well in the centre and pour in the sugar, flavourings and milk. Draw in some of the flour from the sides to mix with these to form a thickish paste. Add the cold fat, cut into small pieces, and cover the whole with more of the flour. Starting from the middle, work all the ingredients quickly with the hands to a firm, smooth paste. If it should stick, cool well through for a time.
Roll out the pastry thinly and cut out different shapes. Brush with the milk and sprinkle with the sugar. Lay the biscuits on a baking sheet and bake till golden.
Oven: pre-heat for 5 minutes at very hot,
bake at moderately hot.
Baking time: 8–10 minutes.

Orange or Lemon Slices

Pastry:
9 oz. (250 g) plain flour
1 level tsp. (3 g) Oetker Baking Powder Backin
2½ oz. (70 g) sugar
1 packet Oetker Vanillin Sugar
1 egg
4½ oz. (125 g) butter or margarine
Filling:
4½ oz. (125 g) almonds (blanched and ground)
5½ oz. (150 g) sugar
juice of 1–2 oranges or lemons
grated rind of one orange or lemon
Icing:
2 well heaped tbsp. icing sugar
about 1 tbsp. orange or lemon juice

For the cake mixture, mix the flour with the Backin and sieve onto a pastry board or cool slab. Make a well in the centre and pour in the sugar, vanillin sugar and egg. Draw in some of the flour from the sides of the well to mix with these ingredients to form a thickish paste. Add the cold fat, cut into small pieces and cover the whole with more of the flour. Starting from the middle, work all these ingredients quickly with the hands into a firm smooth paste. If it should stick, cool well through for a while.
Divide the pastry into halves and roll out each half into a rectangle 12×8 in. (32×22 cm). Place one of the rectangles on a baking sheet.
For the filling, mix the almonds and the sugar with as much orange or lemon juice as will give a spreading consistency. Mix in the grated rind. Spread the filling evenly over the pastry on the baking sheet, leaving about ¼ in. (½ cm) free around the edges. Lay the other pastry rectangle over the filling, press well at the edges and prick with a fork.
Oven: pre-heat for 5 minutes at very hot,
bake at moderately hot.
Baking time: 20–25 minutes.
For the icing, sieve the icing sugar and blend with as much juice as will give a good coating consistency.
Ice the cake as soon as it comes out of the oven and when it has cooled, cut into pieces about ½×2 in. (1×5 cm).

Frisian Biscuits – Light or Dark

Light pastry:
9 oz. (250 g) plain flour
1 level tsp. (3 g) Oetker Baking Powder Backin
3½ oz. (100 g) sugar
1 packet Oetker Vanillin Sugar
1 bottle Oetker rum flavour
2 tbsp. water
3½ oz. (100 g) butter or margarine
or
Dark pastry:
9 oz. (250 g) plain flour
3 level tbsp. cocoa
1 level tsp. (3 g) Oetker Baking Powder Backin
3½ oz. (100 g) sugar
1 packet Oetker Vanillin Sugar
1 bottle Oetker rum flavour
3 tbsp. water
4½ oz. (125 g) butter or margarine
For sprinkling:
coarse-grained sugar

Mix the flour and Backin (and cocoa for the dark mixture) and sieve onto a pastry board or cool slab. Make a well in the centre and pour in the sugar, vanillin sugar, rum flavouring and water. Draw in some of the flour from the sides of the well to mix with these to form a thickish paste. Add the cold fat, cut into small pieces, and cover the whole with more flour. Starting from the middle, work all these ingredients quickly with the hands to a firm, smooth paste. Form 2–3 rolls about 1½ in. (3 cm) thick, roll them in the coarse sugar and cool well through until stiff.
Cut off slices about ¼ in. (½ cm) thick and press the top surface into the sugar. Place on a baking sheet.
Oven: pre-heat for 5 minutes at very hot,
        bake at moderately hot.
Baking time: about 10 minutes.

Ducat Biscuits

Pastry:
9 oz. (250 g) plain flour
1 level tsp. (3 g) Oetker Baking powder Backin
2½ oz. (70 g) sugar
1 packet Oetker Vanillin Sugar
1 egg
1 tbsp. milk or water
4½ oz. (125 g) butter or margarine
Filling:
4½ oz. (125 g) coconut butter
2½ oz. (70 g) icing sugar or castor sugar
1 packet Oetker Vanillin Sugar
1 level tbsp. cocoa
a few drops Oetker rum flavour
1 egg

For the mixture, mix the flour with the Backin and sieve onto a pastry board or cool slab. Make a well in the centre and pour in the sugar, vanillin sugar, egg and milk or water. Draw in some of the flour from the sides of the well to mix with these to form a thickish paste. Add the cold fat, cut into small pieces, and cover the whole with more of the flour. Starting from the middle, work all these ingredients quickly with the hands into a firm smooth paste. If it should stick, cool well through for some time.
Roll out the pastry thinly and cut out round shapes with a pastry cutter, diameter 1.6 in. (4 cm). Place on a greased baking sheet.
Oven: pre-heat for 5 minutes at very hot,
        bake at moderately hot.
Baking time: about 10 minutes.
For the filling, melt the fat and cool it. Put the sugar (sieve icing sugar first), vanillin sugar, sieved cocoa and

Continued on next page

Icing:
2 oz. (55 g) icing sugar
2 level tbsp. cocoa
1–2 tbsp. hot water
½ oz. (15 g) melted butter or margarine

rum flavouring into a mixing bowl and stir in the egg and the lukewarm fat gradually. Leave to cool and when slightly firm sandwich together the biscuits with it. Leave until the filling is quite firm.

For the icing, sieve together the icing sugar and the cocoa and blend with as much of the water as will give a coating consistency. Add the hot fat and coat one half of the top of each biscuit sandwich.

Tea Biscuits (Phot. page 54)

Pastry:
1⅛ lb. (500 g) plain flour
2 level tsp. (6 g) Oetker Baking Powder Backin
5½ oz. (150 g) sugar
1 packet Oetker Vanillin Sugar
2 eggs
9 oz. (250 g) butter or margarine

For decorating:
a little evaporated milk, coarse-grained sugar, almonds (blanched and chopped, sliced or ground)
jam or jelly

For the pastry, mix and sieve together the flour and Backin onto a pastry board or cool slab. Make a well in the centre and pour in the sugar, vanillin sugar and eggs. Draw in some of the flour from the sides of the well to mix with these ingredients to form a thickish paste. Add the cold fat, cut into small pieces and cover the whole with more of the flour. Starting from the middle, work all these ingredients quickly with the hands into a smooth firm paste. If it should stick, cool well through for some time.

Form these different kinds of biscuits from this pastry:

Pretzels: Form the pastry into rolls as thick as a pencil and then make pretzel shapes (see picture) Brush them with milk and dip into the coarse sugar. Lay them on a baking sheet.

Fruit Biscuits: Roll out the pastry thinly and cut out with a pastry cutter round shapes and ring shapes of the same size, lay them on a baking sheet and bake till golden. When they have cooled brush the undersides of the round shapes with jam and lay a ring on top of each. Dust with icing sugar.

Sugar or Nut Biscuits: Roll out the pastry thinly and cut out round shapes with a pastry cutter. Lay them on a baking sheet and brush them over with egg yolk beaten in milk. Sprinkle with coarse sugar or nut and bake till golden.

Filled Biscuits: Roll out the pastry thinly and cut out round shapes with a pastry cutter. Lay them on a baking sheet and bake till golden. When they are cool, brush the undersides of half of them with jam or jelly and place another on top. Dust with icing sugar.

Oven: pre-heat for 5 minutes at very hot, bake at moderately hot.

Baking time: 8–10 minutes.

Salt-Sticks

Pastry:
5 1/2 oz. (150 g) plain flour
3 1/2 oz. (100 g) Oetker Gustin
   (corn starch powder)
2 level tsp. salt
1 egg
3 tbsp. milk
3 1/2 oz. (100 g) butter or margarine
For brushing:
a little tinned milk
For sprinkling:
salt and caraway seeds

Mix together the flour, Gustin and Backin and sieve onto a pastry board or cool slab. Make a well in the centre and pour in the salt, egg and milk. Draw in some of the flour from the sides of the well to mix with these ingredients to form a thickish paste. Add the cold fat, cut into small pieces, and cover the whole with more of the flour. Starting from the middle, work all these ingredients quickly with the hands into a firm, smooth paste. If it should stick, add some more flour.

Roll out the pastry about 0.12 in. (3 mm) thick and cut into strips, 1/2 in. (1 cm) wide and 4 in. (10 cm) long. Brush these with the milk and sprinkle with salt and caraway seeds. A more interesting shape may be obtained if the strips (before being brushed with milk) are twirled into a spiral form i.e. turn one end to the right, the other to the left.

Oven: pre-heat for 5 minutes at very hot,
          bake at moderately hot.
Baking time: about 10 minutes.

Black and White Cookies (Phot. page 92)

Light Pastry:
9 oz. (250 g) plain flour
1 level tsp. (3 g) Oetker Baking
   Powder Backin
5 1/2 oz. (150 g) sugar
1 packet Oetker Vanillin Sugar
1 bottle Oetker rum flavour
1 egg
4 1/2 oz. (125 g) butter or margarine
Dark Pastry:
2 level tbsp. cocoa
1 level tbsp. sugar
1 tbsp. milk
For brushing:
egg white

For the pastry, mix the flour with the Backin and sieve onto a pastry board or cool slab. Make a well in the centre and pour in the sugar, vanillin sugar, flavourings and egg. Draw in some flour from the sides of the well and mix with these ingredients to form a thickish paste. Add the cold fat, cut into small pieces, and cover the whole with more of the flour. Starting from the middle, work all these ingredients quickly with the hands into a firm, smooth paste. If it should stick, cool well through for a time.

Cut the pastry into two halves. Blend together the cocoa, sugar and milk and knead into one of the pastry halves. The two pastries may be combined into the following patterns:

For a pinwheel pattern, roll out two equal-sized rectangles, one in light and one in dark pastry. Brush one over with egg-white and lay the other on top; brush this one with egg-white and roll up like a swiss roll.

For a chequered pattern, roll out the light pastry to a rectangle of 1/2 in. (1 cm) thickness. Cut into 5 strips, each about 1/2 in. (1 cm) wide and of equal length. Roll out the dark pastry to the same size and thickness and

Continued on next page

cut into 4 strips, each 1/2 in. (1 cm) wide and of the same length as the light. Brush them with egg-white and arrange the strips of pastry in three layers of three strips each layer, the colours alternating. Wrap the whole in a thin layer of pastry. The following Black and White Cookies are easier to make: From either the light or dark pastry form rolls about 1 1/2 in. (3 cm) thick. Roll out the other pastry, brush the rolls with egg-white and wrap up in the rolled out pastry.

Cool all the rolls well through until they are stiff, then cut off even slices and place on a greased baking sheet.

Oven: pre-heat for 5 minutes at very hot,
bake at moderately hot.
Baking time: about 10–15 minutes.

Mannheim Biscuits

Pastry:
9 oz. (250 g) plain flour
1 level tsp. (3 g) Oetker Baking Powder Backin
2 1/2 oz. (70 g) sugar
1 packet Oetker Vanillin Sugar
2 egg yolks
4 1/2 oz. (125 g) butter or margarine

Macaroon topping:
2 egg whites
3 oz. (85 g) sugar
4 drops Oetker Baking Essence, bitter almond flavour
4 1/2 oz. (125 g) almonds (blanched or and half ground, half chopped) hazelnuts (half ground, half chopped)

For the mixture, mix the flour with the Backin and sieve onto a pastry board or cool slab. Make a well in the centre and pour in the sugar, vanillin sugar and egg yolks. Draw in some of the flour from the sides of the well and mix with these to form a thickish paste. Add the cold fat, cut into small pieces, and cover the whole with more of the flour. Starting from the middle, work all these ingredients quickly with the hands to a firm, smooth paste. If it should stick, cool well through for some time.

Roll out the pastry about 0.12 in. (3 mm) thick and, using a pastry cutter, cut out round 1.6 in. (4 cm) in diameter.

For the macaroon topping, whisk the egg whites until stiff enough to show and retain a knife cut. Whisk in the sugar gradually, a tablespoon at a time, then add the baking essence. Fold in the almonds or hazelnuts. Spread each biscuit with the topping and place on a baking sheet. If there is not enough topping for all the biscuits, brush the rest with evaporated milk and sprinkle with sugar.

Oven: pre-heat for 5 minutes at very hot,
bake at moderately hot.
Baking time: 10–15 minutes.

Cottage Cheese Pastry (Phot. page 71)

Pastry:
9 oz. (250 g) plain flour
3 level tsp. (9 g) Oetker Baking Powder Backin
1 packet Oetker Vanillin Sugar
9 oz. (250 g) cottage cheese (well pressed out through a cloth to remove surplus moisture, and rubbed through a fine sieve)
7–9 oz. (200–250 g) butter or margarine

Mix the flour and the Backin and sieve onto a pastry board or cool slab. Make a well in the centre and put in the vanillin sugar, cottage cheese and cold fat, cut into small pieces. Cover the fat well over with flour and, starting from the middle, work all these ingredients quickly with the hands to a firm, smooth paste. Roll out the pastry $1/4$ in. ($1/2$ cm) thick, fold together a few times and roll out again. Repeat the folding and rolling out once or twice more and then cool the pastry well through for some time (overnight if possible).

Apple Turnovers

Cottage cheese pastry quantity and method as above
Filling:
$1^{1}/_{8}$ lb. (500 g) apples
$1^{3}/_{4}$ oz. (50 g) sultanas (washed and well drained)
$2^{1}/_{2}$ oz. (70 g) sugar
10 drops Oetker rum flavour
For brushing:
a little evaporated milk
For dusting:
a little icing sugar

For the filling, peel, core and grate the apples and mix with the other ingredients.
Roll out the pastry to $1/4$ in. ($1/2$ cm) thickness and cut out large rounds of 4 in. (10 cm) diameter. Pile some of the filling on to one half of the round and brush the edges with milk. Fold the free half of the round over the filling and press well at the edges. Place on a well-greased baking sheet. Dust with icing sugar when cool.
Oven: pre-heat for 10 minutes at very hot, bake at moderately hot.
Baking time: about 15 minutes.

Coffee Cakes

Pastry:
Cottage cheese pastry quantity and method as above
Filling:
a little jam
Icing: (if desired)
$3^{1}/_{2}$ oz. (100 g) icing sugar
1–2 tbsp. water

Roll out the pastry $1/4$ in. ($1/2$ cm) thick and cut into squares. Place a little jam on each square and fold into different shapes, e.g. triangles, envelopes etc. Rinse a baking sheet with cold water and place the cakes on it.
Oven: pre-heat for 10 minutes at very hot, bake at moderately hot.
Baking time: about 15 minutes.
For the icing, sieve the icing sugar and blend with as much of the water as will give a good coating consistency. Brush over the coffee cakes while they are still warm.

Ham Crescents

Pastry:
Cottage cheese pastry quantity and method see page 70 omitting the vanillin sugar
Filling:
$4^1/2$ oz. (125 g) raw or boiled ham, diced
For brushing:
a little tinned milk

Roll out the pastry thinly and cut out round shapes, the size of a dinner plate. Cut the rounds into halves, then into quarters, then into eighths. Brush over the narrower parts of the segments with milk. Sprinkle a little ham over the middle of the broader end of the segment; roll up from the broader end and form into crescents. Brush with milk. Rinse a baking sheet with cold water and place the ham crescents on it.
Oven: pre-heat for 10 minutes at very hot, bake at moderately hot.
Baking time: 15–20 minutes.

Cheese Biscuits

Pastry:
Cottage cheese pastry quantity and method see page 70
For brushing:
a little tinned milk
For sprinkling:
Parmesan cheese or grated Gruyère cheese
caraway seeds

Roll out the pastry $1/4$ in. ($1/2$ cm) thick. Cut out little strips and squares, brush with milk and sprinkle with the cheese and caraway seeds. Rinse a baking sheet with cold water and place the biscuits on it.
Oven: pre-heat for 5 minutes at very hot, bake at moderately hot.
Baking time: about 10 minutes.
Serve these delicious biscuits with beer or wine. They taste best when fresh.

Mixed Cheese Biscuits

Pastry:
$10^1/2$ oz. (300 g) plain flour
$2^1/2$ oz. (70 g) Oetker Gustin (corn starch powder)
3 level tsp. (9 g) Oetker Baking Powder Backin
$5^1/2$ oz. (150 g) Gruyère cheese (grated), fairly dry
a pinch of paprika
a pinch of pepper
$1/2$ level tsp. salt
1 egg

Mix and sieve together the flour, Gustin and Backin onto a pastry board or cool slab. Stir in the grated Gruyère. Make a well in the centre and pour in the seasonings, egg white, the half egg yolk and liquid. Draw in some of the flour from the sides of the well to mix with these ingredients to form a thickish paste. Add the cold fat, cut into small pieces, and cover the whole with more of the flour. Starting from the middle, work all these ingredients quickly with the hands into a firm, smooth paste. If it should stick, cool well through for a time.
Divide the pastry into 6 equal parts and prepare these 6 different kinds of cheese biscuits.
Continuation s. page 74

1 egg white
½ egg yolk
2 tbsp. milk or water
7 oz. (200 g) butter or margarine
For brushing:
½ egg yolk beaten with 1 tbsp. milk or water
For sprinkling:
coarse-grained salt
caraway seeds
poppy seeds
some grated Parmesan cheese
a little paprika

Cheeselets
Roll out the pastry very thinly. Cut out small round shapes and lay them on a baking sheet. Brush them with the egg yolk, prick well with a fork and sprinkle with salt or caraway seeds.

Cheese Rings
Roll out the pastry thinly and cut out small rings. Lay these on a baking sheet, brush with the egg yolk and sprinkle with poppy seeds.

Cheese Balls
Form the pastry into rolls as thick as a thumb. Cut these into evensized pieces and roll into small balls as big as a cherry. Using a Oetker Baking Essence bottle, make a little well in the middle of each. Place the balls on a baking sheet, brush with egg yolk and sprinkle a little Parmesan cheese in the well.

Pretzels
Make very thin rolls of the pastry about 6 in. (15 cm) long and thinner than a pencil. Form these into pretzel shapes, brush with egg yolk and dip the brushed surface of some in poppy seeds or caraway seeds before placing on a baking sheet.

Cheese Crescents
Roll out the pastry thinly and cut out rounds, the size of a tea plate, about 8 in. (20 cm) in diameter. Brush with egg yolk and sprinkle with Parmesan cheese and a little paprika. Cut the rounds first into halves, then into quarters, then into eighths. Roll up each triangle into a crescent, starting from the outside and curving it slightly. Brush with egg yolk.

Cheese Straws
Roll out the pastry a good 0.1 in. (2 mm) thick. Use a pastry wheel if possible to cut out strips ½ in. (1 cm) wide and 3¼ in. (8 cm) long. Lay these on a baking sheet, brush with egg yolk and sprinkle with caraway seeds. Make more interesting shape by twirling the strips, before brushing with egg yolk, into spirals, turning one end to the right, the other to the left.

Oven: pre-heat for 5 minutes at very hot, bake at moderately hot.

Baking time: about 10 minutes.

THE "FIVE MINUTES" PASTRY

IMPORTANT PREPARATIONS

1. When shopping remember that cottage cheese should be soft in texture and snow-white in colour. Its taste should be slightly sour.
Press very soft cottage cheese in a firm cloth (to remove surplus moisture) before weighing. If the recipe requires it, rub through a fine sieve.
2. Mix together the flour and Backin and sieve them. This mixing and sieving loosens the flour, thus aerating it. It also distributes the baking powder evenly throughout the flour, making for a lighter cake.
3. For this pastry baking sheets and cake forms should be greased. Use soft butter or margarine for this and apply carefully and evenly with a pastry brush.

PASTRY MIXING METHOD

Mix the cottage cheese with the milk, egg, oil, sugar, vanillin sugar and salt, according to the recipe. Mix and sieve together the flour and the Backin and add to the mixed ingredients, a little at a time, until slightly more than half has been used. Knead the rest of the flour into the mixture.

FOUR SIMPLE STEPS

1. **Mix the cottage cheese with the milk and with the egg, oil, sugar, vanillin sugar and salt, according to the recipe . . . .**
Place the ingredients, in the order given in the recipe, in a mixing bowl (preferably of stoneware, earthenware or china). Break the egg into a cup first to ensure that it is fresh.

The oil plays an important part in the success of this pastry and a hard fat should not be substituted. Any kind of salad oil which has no pronounced taste may be used. For mixing use a wooden spoon with a hole in it; hold it so that the handle is perpendicular and grip it as far down the handle as possible. Mix in an anticlockwise direction until all the ingredients are combined into a smooth mass.

Cottage Cheese Pastry   Recipe page 67
Cream Puffs   Recipe page 138

2. **Mix and sieve together the flour and the Backin and add to the mixed ingredients, a little at a time, until slightly more than half of it has been used. . . .**
Stir in the flour and baking powder until no more flour can be seen.

3. **Knead the rest of the flour into the mixture.**
Tip the rest of the flour and baking powder onto a pastry board or cool slab and empty the pastry mixture onto it. Cover with flour and, starting from the middle, knead the whole quickly into a smooth paste (see pictures page 41/7a-c).

4. **Many different types of cakes and savouries can be made from this pastry. It can be rolled out, cut into shapes and filled, or be given some kind of topping.**
For small cakes, roll out the pastry $1/4$ in. ($1/2$ cm) thick, divide into squares and place a little jam in the middle of each. Fold the pieces into different shapes, e.g. triangles and rectangles and turnovers Brush with milk and bake on a greased baking sheet.

BAKING "FIVE MINUTES PASTRY"

Bake all cakes and savouries according to the instructions in the recipe. After removing from the oven, loosen the cake from the tin or baking sheet and place on a cake wire to cool. Cakes and savouries baked from this pastry taste best when fresh.

CAKES IN BAKING TINS

Bienenstich

Pastry:
3½ oz. (100 g) cottage cheese (well pressed out)
4 tbsp. milk
4 tbsp. oil
2 well heaped tbsp. sugar
a pinch of salt
7 oz. (200 g) plain flour
4 level tsp. Oetker Baking Powder Backin

Topping:
1¾–2½ oz. (50–75 g) butter
3½ oz. (100 g) sugar
1 packet Oetker Vanillin Sugar
1 tbsp. milk
3½ oz. (100 g) almonds (blanched and thinly sliced)

For the pastry, rub the cottage cheese, if desired, through a fine sieve and mix with the milk, oil, sugar and salt. Mix and sieve together the flour and the Backin and add to the mixed ingredients, a little at a time, until slightly more than half has been used. Knead in the rest of the flour. Grease a round cake tin with a removable rim, 10 in. (26 cm) in diameter and roll out the pastry to fit the base.

For the topping, melt together the butter, sugar and vanillin sugar and add the milk; stir in the almonds and set aside to cool. If it should be too firm when cold, add a little milk. Spread evenly over the pastry.

Oven: moderately hot.

Baking time: about 20 minutes.

Alternatively the cake may be filled with buttercream, made from ½ packet Oetker Pudding Powder, Vanilla Flavour, 2 well heaped tbsp. sugar, ½ pt. cold milk and 3½ oz. (100 g) butter or margarine. When the cake is quite cold, cut it horizontally into two halves, spread the filling on the bottom half and lay the other on top.

Cottage Cheese and Oil Pastry (1)

Pastry:
5½ oz. (150 g) cottage cheese (well pressed out)
6 tbsp. milk
6 tbsp. oil
2½ oz. (75 g) sugar
1 packet Oetker Vanillin Sugar
a pinch of salt
10½ oz. (300 g) plain flour
1 packet Oetker Baking Powder Backin

Rub the cottage cheese through a fine sieve, if desired, and mix with the milk, oil, sugar, vanillin sugar and salt. Mix and sieve together the flour and the Backin and add to the mixed ingredients, a little at a time, until slightly more than half has been used. Knead in the rest of the flour.

Cottage Cheese and Oil Pastry (2)

Pastry:
7 oz. (200 g) cottage cheese
  (well pressed out)
6 tbsp. milk
1 egg
8 tbsp. oil
3½ oz. (100 g) sugar
1 packet Oetker Vanillin Sugar
a pinch of salt
14 oz. (400 g) plain flour
1 packet and 2 level tsp. Oetker
  Baking Powder Backin

Rub the cottage cheese through a fine sieve, if desired, and mix with the milk, egg oil, sugar, vanillin sugar and salt. Mix and sieve together the flour and the Backin and add to the mixed ingredients, a little at a time, until slightly more than half has been used. Knead in the rest of the flour.

Cottage Cheese and Oil Pastry (3)

Pastry:
4½ oz. (125 g) cottage cheese
  (well pressed out)
4 tbsp. milk
1 egg yolk
½ egg white
4 tbsp. oil
1 level tsp. salt
9 oz. (250 g) plain flour
1 packet Oetker Baking Powder Backin

Rub the cottage cheese through a fine sieve, if desired, and mix with the milk, egg yolk and ½ egg white, oil and salt. Mix and sieve together the flour and the Backin and add to the mixed ingredients, a little at a time, until slightly more than half has been used. Knead in the rest of the flour.
The following cakes and savouries may be made from these three kinds of pastry.

Rose Cake

Pastry:
cottage cheese and oil pastry (2)
method and quantity see above
For brushing the pastry:
2½ oz. (75 g) soft butter or margarine
Filling:
2 well heaped tbsp. sugar
1 packet Oetker Vanillin Sugar
2½ oz. (75 g) currants
  (washed and well drained)
2½ oz. (75 g) sultanas
  (washed and well drained)
3½ oz. (100 g) almonds
  (blanched and finely chopped)
For brushing the cake surface:
a little tinned milk

Roll out the pastry to a rectangle 20 × 15 in. (50 × 40 cm) and brush with the soft fat. Sprinkle evenly with the ingredients for the filling and roll up like a swiss roll, starting from the longer side. Cut the roll into 15 equal pieces. Grease a round cake tin with a removable rim, diameter 10 in. (26 cm) and place the pastry pieces upright in it. Brush the surface with milk.
Oven: moderately hot.
Baking time: 35–55 minutes.

Hedgehog Roll

Pastry:
Cottage cheese and oil pastry (2) method and quantity see page 80
For brushing the pastry:
3½ oz. (100 g) soft butter or margarine
Filling:
3½ oz. (100 g) candied lemon peel (diced)
3½ oz. (100 g) almonds (blanched and finely chopped)
5½ oz. (150 g) sultanas (washed and well drained)
2 well heaped tbsp. sugar
1 packet Oetker Vanillin Sugar
1 level tsp. ground cinnamon
1 bottle Oetker rum flavour
3 drops Oetker Baking Essence, bitter almond flavour
For brushing the roll:
a little milk
Icing:
5½ oz. (150 g) icing sugar
1–2 tbsp. hot water
For decorating:
about ½ oz. (15 g) almonds (blanched and cut lengthways into spikes)

Roll out the pastry to a rectangle 30 × 12 in. (80 × 30 cm) and brush with the fat.
For the filling, combine together all the ingredients for the filling and distribute evenly over the pastry surface. Roll up like a swiss roll, starting from the long side. Grease a round cake tin with a removable rim, diameter 10 in. (26 cm). Lay the roll in the cake tin in a spiral shape and brush with milk.
Oven: moderately hot.
Baking time: about 50 minutes.
For the icing sieve the icing sugar and blend with as much water as will give a good coating consistency. Ice the roll and decorate with the almond 'spikes'.

CAKES ON A BAKING SHEET

Gundula Ring

Pastry:
Cottage cheese and oil pastry (2) method and quantity see page 80
For brushing the pastry:
1³/₄ oz. (50 g) soft butter or margarine
Filling:
3¹/₂ oz. (100 g) candied lemon peel (diced)
3¹/₂ oz. (100 g) almonds (blanched and finely chopped)
5¹/₂ oz. (150 g) sultanas (washed and well drained)
2 well heaped tbsp. sugar
1 packet Oetker Vanillin Sugar
1 level tsp. ground cinnamon
1 bottle Oetker rum flavour
3 drops Oetker Baking Essence, bitter almond flavour
For brushing the ring:
a little tinned milk

If the pastry should be rather soft knead in a little more (up to 1³/₄ oz. (50 g)) flour. Then roll out the pastry to a rectangle of 20 × 22 in. (about 50 × 55 cm). Brush with the fat and cut lengthways into two halves.
For the filling, combine the ingredients for the filling and distribute over the two pieces of pastry so that, at the cut edge of each a border of 1 in. (2 cm) is left free of filling. Roll up each piece of pastry, starting from the outer long edge. Entwine the two rolls together and lay as a ring on a greased baking sheet. Brush with milk and make cuts ¹/₂ in. (1 cm) deep in the surface.
Oven: moderately hot.
Baking time: about 30 minutes.

Apple or Plum Cake

Pastry:
Cottage cheese and oil pastry (1) method and quantity see page 79
Fruit topping:
2¹/₄–3¹/₄ lb. (1–1¹/₂ kg) apples or plums
For sprinkling:
a little sugar

Roll out the pastry onto a greased baking sheet.
For the fruit topping, peel and core the apples and cut into slices or quarters (if the apples are very large divide into eighths). If plums are used, rub them clean, then stone. Distribute the fruit evenly over the pastry, lay plums with the inside upwards. Fold a piece of greased paper a number of times and lay it against the pastry at the open side of the baking sheet.
Oven: pre-heat for 5 minutes at very hot, bake at moderately hot.
Baking time: 15–25 minutes.
After baking, when the cake has cooled somewhat, sprinkle with sugar.

Nut or Almond Ring

Pastry:
Cottage cheese and oil pastry (1) method and quantity see page 79
Filling:
7 oz. (200 g) ground hazelnuts
or
7 oz. (200 g) almonds
   (blanched and ground)
3½ oz. (100 g) sugar
4–5 drops Oetker Baking Essence,
   bitter almond flavour
1 egg white
½ egg yolk
3–4 tbsp. water
For brushing:
½ egg yolk beaten with 1 tbsp. milk

Roll out the pastry to a rectangle 14 × 18 in. (35 × 45 cm).
For the filling, mix the nuts, sugar, baking essence, egg white and ½ egg yolk with as much of the water as will give a good spreading consistency and spread evenly over the pastry with a spatula. Starting from the longer side, roll up the pastry like a swiss roll; form the roll into a ring and lay on a greased baking sheet. Brush with the egg yolk and make regular cuts in the surface ¼ in. (½ cm) deep.
Oven: moderately hot.
Baking time: about 20 minutes.

SMALL CAKES

Apple Turnovers

Pastry:
Cottage cheese and oil pastry (1) method and quantity see page 79
Filling:
1⅛–1¾ lb. (500–750 g) apples
1¾–2½ oz. (50–75 g) sugar
1¾ oz. (50 g) sultanas
   (washed and well drained)
3–4 drops Oetker Baking Essence,
   lemon flavour
For brushing:
a little milk
Icing:
3½ oz. (100 g) icing sugar
1–2 tbsp. hot water

For the filling, peel and core the apples and cut into pieces. Add the sugar and the sultanas and stew for a short time over a slow heat, stirring all the time. Cool well through, sweeten to taste, then add the baking essence.
Roll out the pastry thinly and cut out round shapes 4 in. (10 cm) in diameter. Pile some of the filling onto one half of the round and brush the edges thinly with milk. Fold over the free half of the round and use a baking essence bottle to press the edges well together. Lay on a greased baking sheet.
Oven: moderately hot.
Baking time: about 15 minutes.
For the icing, sieve the icing sugar and blend with as much of the water as will give a good coating consistency. Brush the turnovers with the icing as soon as they come out of the oven.

Sausage Rolls

Pastry:
Cottage cheese and oil pastry (3) method and quantity see page 80
Filling:
$1/2$ egg white
12 sausages about 6 in. (16 cm) long
For brushing:
a little tinned milk

Roll out the pastry $1/8$ in. (3 mm) thick; with a pastry wheel cut out 12 rectangles of 6×4 in. (16×10 cm) and brush the edges with egg white. Roll up a sausage in each piece of pastry and lay on a greased baking sheet. Brush with milk.
Oven: pre-heat for 5 minutes at very hot, bake at moderately hot.
Baking time: 15–20 minutes.

Currant Wheels

Pastry:
Cottage cheese and oil pastry (1) method and quantity see page 79
For brushing:
1 oz. (30 g) soft butter or margarine
Filling:
2 well heaped tbsp. sugar
1 packet Oetker Vanillin Sugar
$1^3/4$ oz. (50 g) currants
 (washed and well drained)
$2^1/2$ oz. (70 g) sultanas
 (washed and well drained)
$1^3/4$ oz. (50 g) almonds
 (blanched and finely chopped)
Icing:
6 oz. (170 g) icing sugar
about 2 tbsp. hot water

Roll out the pastry to a rectangle 14×18 in. (45×35 cm) and brush with the fat.
For the filling, mix together the filling ingredients and distribute evenly over the pastry. Starting from the shorter side, roll up like a swiss roll. Then use a sharp knife to cut off slices about $1^1/4$ in. ($1^1/2$ cm) thick. Lay these on a greased baking sheet and flatten slightly.
Oven: pre-heat for 5 minutes at very hot, bake at very hot.
Baking time: 15–20 minutes.
For the icing, sieve the icing sugar, and blend with as much of the water as will give a good coating consistency. Ice the currant wheels while still hot.

Ham Rolls

Pastry:
Cottage cheese and oil pastry (3) method and quantity see page 80
For brushing:
½ egg white
Filling:
2½ oz. (70 g) raw ham
2½ oz. (70 g) boiled ham
2 small pickled gherkins
For brushing:
a little tinned milk

Roll out the pastry thinly and cut out rectangles of 3 × 6 in. (7 × 14 cm). Brush the edges of these with egg white.
For the filling, cut the ham and the gherkins into strips of 3 in. (7 cm) long. Place a few strips of ham and gherkins on each piece of pastry and roll up from the shorter side. Lay the rolls on a greased baking sheet and brush with milk.
Oven: pre-heat for 5 minutes at very hot, bake at very hot.
Baking time: about 15 minutes.

Hunter's Buns

Pastry:
Cottage cheese and oil pastry (1) method and quantity see page 79
2½ oz. (75 g) currants
 (washed and well drained)
For brushing:
a little tinned milk

Knead the currants lightly into the pastry and form it into a roll. Divide into 16 equal-sized pieces; form these into round bun shapes, lay on a greased baking sheet and brush with milk.
Oven: moderately hot.
Baking time: about 20 minutes.
Alternatively, the buns may be filled with jam. To do this, flattern the buns slightly and place ½ tsp. jam in the centre of each. Gather the edges together over the jam and press well together. Turn them over, with the round side to the top and lay on a greased baking sheet.

Savoury Snacks

Pastry:
4½ oz. (125 g) cottage cheese
 (well pressed out)
4 tbsp. milk
1 egg
4 tbsp. oil
9 oz. (250 g) plain flour
1 packet Oetker Baking Powder Backin
Filling:
4½ oz. (125 g) raw ham
 (cut into thin slices)
2¼ oz. (65 g) herb-flavoured cheese
 (cut up small)
For brushing:
a little tinned milk

For the pastry, rub the cottage cheese through a fine sieve, if desired, and mix with the milk, egg and oil. Mix and sieve together the flour and the Backin and add to the mixed ingredients, a little at a time until slightly more than half has been used. Knead in the rest of the flour. Roll out the pastry to a square about 16 × 16 in. (36 × 36 cm) and cut into 4 in. (9 cm) squares with a pastry wheel. Distribute some of the ham and cheese over the surface of each square and roll up, pressing the edges firmly. Lay the snacks on a greased baking sheet and brush with milk.
Oven: pre-heat for 5 minutes at very hot, bake at moderately hot.
Baking time: about 20 minutes.

IMPORTANT PREPARATIONS

1. Prepare the hazelnuts or almonds according to instructions for "Cakes made by the Creaming method" (see page 10).
2. To bake this sponge mixture, line the base of baking sheets and cake tins with paper (see illustrations).
   a) For a round cake tin, prepare the lining as follows: turn over the tin, bottom upwards, and lay some plain paper on it; use greaseproof if possible. Cut away the extra paper round the base with a knife.
   b) Greasing the tin; use a pastry brush to apply soft butter or margarine to four different parts of the base. Do NOT grease the rim.
   c) Line the base with the paper and press well against it.

CAKE MIXING METHOD

Separate the eggs whites from the yolks. Whisk the yolks with the water until frothy, then add $2/3$ of the sugar and the vanillin sugar, a little at a time. Continue whisking until the mixture is thick and creamy. Add the flavourings. Whisk the egg whites in a separate bowl until stiff enough to show and retain the cut of a knife: gradually whisk in the rest of the sugar. Fill the egg white snow onto the whisked egg yolk mixture. Mix together the flour, the Gustin and the Backin and sieve onto the egg whites. Fold all gently together (do not stir or beat!). Line a cake tin or baking sheet with paper and fill the cake mixture into it.

SEVEN SIMPLE STEPS

1. "Separate the egg whites from the yolks...."
Break each egg first into a cup to ensure that it is fresh. Separate the yolks from the whites carefully; the egg whites cannot be really stiffly whisked if they contain even a small scrap of yolk. The egg whites should not be whisked too early – only when the recipe requires it.

2. "... Whisk the yolks with the water until frothy ..."
Add the water to the egg yolks. The amount of water necessary depends on the size of the eggs; if the eggs used are rather small use the larger amount of water if a choice is given in the recipe; if they are large, take the smaller amount.
The egg yolks should be whisked energetically until the mass falls in thick drops from the whisk. The whisk used should be really efficient if this sponge is to be made quickly and successfully.

3. "...Then add ²/₃ of the sugar with the vanillin sugar, a little at a time. Continue whisking until the mixture is thick and creamy. Add the flavourings.."
The sugar should not be added all at once but a little at a time, while whisking constantly. The mixture is "thick and creamy" when the rings which fall from the whisk when held above the mixture do not disappear immediately but stay visible for a short

time. Add the flavourings when the egg yolk mixture is ready whisked.

4. "...Whisk the egg whites in a separate bowl until stiff enough to show and retain the cut of a knife, then gradually whisk in the rest of the sugar.."
This whisked sponge can only succeed if the egg white is whipped really stiff. First, whisk the egg white without sugar into a firm snow; to test if it is stiff enough, draw the wire whisk out of the snow and turn it round; if the points of snow, which before hung under the whisk, now remain pointing upwards, then the mass is stiff enough. Whisk the sugar gradually into the egg white snow by adding a tbsp. of sugar and then whisking so long until a cut with a clean knife remains visible (or use the test with the whisk, mentioned above). This whisking must be repeated after each addition of sugar otherwise the egg white will become liquid.

5. "... Fill the egg white snow onto the whisked egg yolk mixture. Mix together the flour, the Gustin and the Backin and sieve onto the egg whites...."
The mixing and sieving loosens and aerate the flour and distributes the Gustin (blancmange powder, cocoa) and Backin evenly throughout. This makes for a lighter cake. If dried fruit is mentioned in the recipe, sprinkle over the flour.

6. "... **Fold all the ingredients gently together (do not stir or beat!)...**"

In order not to spoil the consistency of the egg snow the ingredients must on no account be beaten in. Use this method to absorb the flour: draw the wire whisk over the base, from one side to the other through the mixture; lift the whisk out of the mixture and shake lightly to empty. The ingredients are sufficiently folded together when no more flour is visible. This folding in must be completed fairly speedily otherwise the egg snow will collapse.

7. "... **Line a cake tin or baking sheet with paper and fill the cake mixture into it...**"

Use, if possible, a plastic scraper to fill the sponge mixture into the prepared tin. Level it evenly.

THE BAKING OF WHISKED SPONGE

Cakes of this mixture must be baked immediately after being prepared otherwise the egg white snow will collapse. Each should be baked according to the instructions in the recipe. Always test whether the cake is baked through before removing from the oven; lay the flat of the hand lightly on the surface; it should not feel damp, and the cake surface should be soft and cotton-wool like. Allow to cool slightly then loosen from the sides of the tin with a knife and remove the rim. Turn onto a cake wire so that the cake can dry off and for the same reason remove the paper from the base of the cake. If however the cake is not be used that day, leave the paper on until later.

CAKES IN BAKING TINS

Rum Sponge Cake

Sponge mixture:
3 eggs
3 tbsp. warm water
5^1/$_2$ oz. (150 g) sugar
1 packet Oetker Vanillin Sugar
1 bottle Oetker rum flavour
2 drops Oetker Baking Essence, bitter almond flavour
a pinch of salt
5^1/$_2$ oz. (150 g) plain flour
5 slightly heaped tbsp. Oetker Gustin (corn starch powder)
or
1 packet Oetker Pudding Powder, vanilla flavour
1^1/$_2$ level tsp. (4^1/$_2$ g) Oetker Baking Powder Backin
2^1/$_2$ oz. (70 g) butter or margarine (melted)

Icing:
4^1/$_2$ oz. (125 g) icing sugar
3 level tbsp. cocoa
1–2 tbsp. hot water
if desired ^{3}/$_4$ oz. (20 g) coconut butter (melted)

For the sponge mixture, whisk the eggs with the water until frothy, then gradually add the sugar and the vanillin sugar. Continue whisking until the mixture is thick and creamy. Whisk in the flavourings. Mix together the flour, the Gustin (pudding powder) and Backin and sieve over the mixture. Fold all the ingredients gently together (do not stir or beat), adding gradually at the same time the cooled fat. Grease a loaf cake tin and line with paper. Fill in the cake mixture and bake immediately.
Oven: moderately hot.
Baking time: 40–50 minutes.
For the icing, sieve together the icing sugar and the cocoa and blend with as much of the water as will give a good coating consistency. Add the hot fat and ice the cooled cake.

Mandarine Slices

Cake mixture:
2 egg yolks
2–3 tbsp. warm water*
3½ oz. (100 g) sugar
1 packet Oetker Vanillin Sugar
2 egg whites
2½ oz. (70 g) plain flour
1¾ oz. (50 g) Oetker Gustin
(corn starch powder)
1 level tsp. (3 g) Oetker Baking Powder Backin

Butter cream filling:
½ packet Oetker Pudding Powder, vanilla flavour
1¾ oz. (50 g) sugar
½ pt. (285 ccm) cold milk
4½ oz. (125 g) butter or margarine

For decorating:
1⅛–1¾ lb. (500–750 g) mandarine segments (tinned)

Glaze:
1 packet Oetker Cake Glaze, transparent
1 well heaped tbsp. sugar

For sprinkling:
1¾ oz. (50 g) grated chocolate

* If the eggs are rather large, take the smaller quantity of water; if they are small, take the larger.

For the cake mixture, whisk the egg yolks and water until frothy, then whisk in gradually ⅔ of the sugar and the vanillin sugar. Continue whisking until the mixture is thick and creamy. Whisk the egg whites until stiff enough to show and retain a knife cut, then whisk in gradually the rest of the sugar. Pile the egg white snow onto the egg yolk cream. Sieve onto these the flour, Backin and Gustin, then fold all gently together (do not stir or beat). Line a loaf baking tin with greaseproof paper; fill the cake mixture into and bake immediately.
Oven: moderately hot.
Baking time: 20–30 minutes.
Allow the sponge to cool well through.
For the butter cream filling, blend the pudding powder and the sugar with 3 tbsp. of the milk. Bring the rest of the milk to the boil; remove from heat and stir in the blended pudding powder mixture. Boil up briefly, then cool, stirring occasionally.
Cream the fat and beat in the pudding, a tbsp. at a time, taking care that neither pudding nor fat are too cool otherwise the mixture may curdle.
Cut the sponge through twice.
Drain the mandarine segments well and measure of ½ pt. (285 ccm) of the syrup. Cover the top and bottom sponge layers with the mandarine segments. Prepare the cake glaze according to the instructions on the packet, cool for one minute then spoon carefully over the fruit, placing the middle sponge layer (without fruit) on the lower fruit covered layer. When the glaze has set spread a good half of the buttercream filling evenly over the middle sponge layer and cover with the top layer. Coat the sides of the cake with the rest of the filling and sprinkle with the chocolate.

Strawberry Cream Cake　Recipe page 112
Fruit Flan　Recipe page 25 + 44
Fruit Tartlets　Recipe page 56

Flana-filled Sponge

Sponge mixture:
2 eggs
1 tbsp. warm water
3½ oz. (100 g) sugar
1 packet Oetker Vanillin Sugar
2½ oz. (70 g) plain flour
5 slightly heaped tbsp. Oetker Gustin (corn starch powder)
1 level tsp. (3 g) Oetker Baking Powder Backin
1¾ oz. (50 g) butter or margarine

Butter cream filling:
1 packet Oetker Chocolate Pudding Powder Flana
2 well heaped tbsp. sugar
4 tbsp. cold milk for blending
½ pt. (285 ccm) milk
5½ oz. (150 g) butter or margarine
¾ oz. (20 g) coconut butter (melted)

For decorating:
2 oz. (60 g) chocolate vermicelli

For the sponge mixture, whisk the eggs with the water until frothy, then gradually add the sugar and the vanillin sugar; continue whisking until the mixture is thick and creamy. Mix together the flour, the Gustin and the Backin and sieve over the mixture. Fold all the ingredients gently together – do not stir or beat –, at the same time adding the cooled fat gradually. Grease a loaf cake tin and line with paper. Fill into it the sponge mixture and bake immediately.
Oven: moderately hot.
Baking time: about 30 minutes.
For the butter cream filling, mix the contents of the packet and the sugar well together in a cup; add 2 tbsp. milk and beat well with a fork until all lumps have disappeared, then add the remaining 2 tbsp. milk. Bring the ½ pt. (285 ccm) milk to the boil; remove from heat and stir in the blended Flana mixture slowly; return to heat and boil up for a minute. Set aside to cool, stirring now and again. Cream the fat and beat in the cooled Flana, a tbsp. at a time (take care that neither the fat nor Flana are too cool otherwise the cream may curdle). Finally beat in the hot coconut butter.
Cut the cold sponge through horizontally and spread a little more than half the butter cream over the lower half. Lay the upper half on top. Spoon 3 well heaped tbsp. cream into a forcing bag and spread the rest of the cream evenly over the cake; coat the sides with the chocolate vermicelli. Decorate the cake with the butter cream in the forcing bag.

Apple or Cherry Sponge Cake Recipe page 21
Black and White Cookies Recipe page 65

FILLING AND DECORATING LARGE CAKES

FILLING THE CAKE

1. Lay the sponge cake on a piece of paper so that the bottom, which is usually smoother, is now on the top. The cake may be cut through with a strong thread, or a long knife. In order to ensure that the layers are of equal thickness, cut $1/2$ in. (1 cm) deep into the cake all the way round with a small sharp knife.

2. Lay a strong thread in this cut all the way around, take the two ends and cross them; pull firmly and the thread will cut through the cake.

3. Lift the layer of cake off with a piece of paper so that it will not break. To do this, crease a piece of paper downwards and place the crease between the layers; push gently between the layers, the index fingers holding the top layer now and again so that the paper can be slid between.

4. The top layer may now be lifted off.

5. If the cake is to be cut with a knife, use one that is longer than the cake diameter.

6. The usual fillings are butter cream, made with Oetker Pudding Powder, or jam. Or the cake may be filled once with cream and once with jam. The filling may be spread on with a spatula or a palette or dinner knife.

7. When the bottom layer has been spread with the filling, carefully slip the middle layer from the paper onto the filling. It is important that it should fit exactly on top, edge above edge all the way round.

8. Spread filling evenly over this layer and place the top layer carefully on it.

DECORATING CAKES

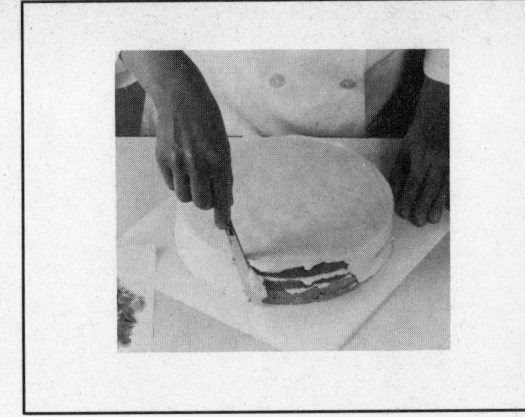

1. The cake should be spread with butter cream around the sides and on the top. Use a dinner knife to smooth the cream evenly round the sides.

2. The sides may be coated with chocolate vermicelli, halved almonds, ground hazelnuts or browned rolled oats. Place the coating ingredients on the paper close to the cake and lift up against the sides with a plastic scraper or knife.

3. Before piping on the butter cream decoration, divide the top surface into equal pieces with a strong thread.

4. When piping, remember that the forcing bag should be held at right angles to the cake. The right hand should hold the bag shut and simultaneously squeeze out the cream necessary. The left hand should guide the bag, but with the thumb and index finger only touching it above the nozzle, not the whole hand, otherwise the hand warmth could melt the cream and it could not be piped accurately.

5. Remove the finished cake from the paper onto a cake plate. To do this slide a palette knife under it and support it with the left hand so that it does not break.

PIPING DECORATIONS

Butter cream may be piped in many different patterns onto the cake, but this piping demands some skill. Therefore practise first using soft mashed potatoes before trying the cream. The following patterns have proved most popular.

SOME DECORATED CAKES

1. Here the decoration consists of stars of different sizes; they graduate from larger round the edge to smaller in the middle. Tiny blobs of jelly placed in the middle of the stars of the inner and outer ring bring some colour into the cake's attractive appearence.

2. A criss cross pattern is piped over it in butter cream and an edging of rosettes complete the picture.

3. Here wavy lines are piped sideways from the middle outwards, the waves increasing in size towards the outside. A star piped at the outer rim finishes off each wavy line.

4. In this case the wavy line "stands up" i.e. the waves have been piped at right angles to the cake, against each other. Each wave ends with a half rosette and the middle is emphasized by a ring of little stars.

5. Here is a "butterfly cake". The edging consists of rosettes piped very close together. Then another, looser rosette is piped onto each cake segment. Two halves of an unblanched almond are stuck into each as "wings" and the longish body can be shown with jelly or "hundreds and thousands". A ring of small rosettes encircles the middle.

6. This cone effect can be achieved by piping loops from the middle, very close together, increasing in size towards the outer edge. The cones are finished off with a cherry or a little jam or jelly is piped inside each.

7. Here a "sunflower cake" is shown. The middle is sprinkled with chocolate vermicelli and enclosed with a ring of stars, piped close together and each lengthened by a "tail" pointing towards the outer edge. The edging here is made by piping rings so that they lie sideways.

8. In this cake decoration the wavy line has been effectively used. Instead of being piped at right angles, in one line, the piping tube has been turned slightly to the left or the right after each up and down movement. Each cake segment has been shown by a small "standing up" wavy line which finishes in a point towards the middle.

9. Here the middle of the cake has been first spread with jam, then a trellis work pattern has been piped over it, enclosed by a ring of little stars. The edging is made up of loops, pipes close to each other, which have been looped alternately to the left and to the right.

10. "Sixes" have been used most effectively to decorate the edges of this cake. They have been piped as close to each other as possible. First pipe a six, then pipe backwards round the o of the six, then start the next six — all this without removing the piping tube from the cake. Each segment is marked by two rings piped on top of each other and towards the middle a star lengthened into a tail pointing towards the middle. In each ring a cherry may be laid, or pipe a little jelly inside.

ICING CAKES

1. Coat the cake thinly with jam before icing – this prevents the icing from sinking into the cake. Use a smooth jam of course; apricot is most suitable under white icing. If the jam has seeds or fruit pieces, rub through a sieve first.

2. Pour the icing onto the middle of the cake.

3. Spread the icing quickly over the surface with a large knife and allow to run down the sides. Hold the knife so that the blade is slanting and do not press heavily. Change the spreading direction without lifting the knife from the icing, as this could remove crumbs from the cake surface and the smooth appearance of the icing would be spoilt.

4. The icing running down the sides should be smoothed upwards using a knife held so that the blade is slanting.

5. The cake can be decorated with halved almonds (hazelnuts), but the icing must be still wet otherwise they will not stick, so this decorating must be done very quickly. It is also important that the cake should be moved as quickly as possible onto a cake plate or else the icing will crack; or, alternatively, the cake can be left on the paper until the icing is completely dry, and then moved.

Sponge Cakes, suitable for filling with butter cream or whipped cream

Sponge mixture (1):
2 egg yolks, 2–3 tbsp. warm water*
3½ oz. (100 g) sugar
1 packet Oetker Vanillin Sugar
2 egg whites
2½ oz. (70 g) plain flour
5 slightly heaped tbsp. Oetker Gustin (corn starch powder)
1 level tsp. (3 g) Oetker Baking Powder Backin

Sponge mixture (2):
3 egg yolks, 3–4 tbsp. warm water*
5½ oz. (150 g) sugar
1 packet Oetker Vanillin Sugar
3 egg whites
3½ oz. (100 g) plain flour
3½ oz. (100 g) Oetker Gustin (corn starch powder)
3 level tsp. (9 g) Oetker Baking Powder Backin

Sponge mixture (3):
4 egg yolks, 2 tbsp. warm water*
5½ oz. (150 g) sugar
1 packet Oetker Vanillin Sugar
4 egg whites
3½ oz. (100 g) plain flour
3½ oz. (100 g) Oetker Gustin (corn starch powder)
2 level tsp. (6 g) Oetker Baking Powder Backin

Sponge mixture (4):
4 egg yolks, 3–4 tbsp. warm water*
6 oz. (70 g) sugar
1 packet Oetker Vanillin Sugar
4 egg whites
3½ oz. (100 g) plain flour
3½ oz. (100 g) Oetker Gustin (corn starch powder)
3 level tbsp. cocoa
3 level tsp. (9 g) Oetker Baking Powder Backin

* If the eggs are rather large, take the smaller quantity of water; if they are small, take the larger.

Whisk the egg yolks with the water until frothy, then add ⅔ of the sugar and the vanillin sugar, a little at a time; continue whisking until the mixture is thick and creamy. Whisk the egg whites in a separate bowl until stiff enough to show and retain the cut of a knife, then gradually whisk in the rest of the sugar. Fill the egg white snow onto the whisked egg yolk mixture. Mix together the flour, the Gustin (for sponge mixture (4) the cocoa too) and the Backin and sieve onto the egg whites. Fold all the ingredients gently together (do not stir or beat). Line the base of a round cake tin with a removable rim, diameter 10 in. (26 cm) with paper and fill into it the sponge mixture. Bake immediately.

Oven: moderately hot.
Baking time: 20–30 minutes.
Cool the cake well through.

Wine Cream-filled Sponge Cake

1 cake using Sponge mixture (1) see page 106
Filling:
1 packet Oetker Regina Gelatine, ground white
3 tbsp. cold water for blending
almost 1/2 pt. (285 ccm) water
1 packet Oetker Fruttina Pudding Powder, lemon flavour
4 1/2 oz. (125 g) sugar
almost 1/2 pt. (285 ccm) hock or similar white wine
1 tbsp. lemon juice
2/3 pt. (375 ccm) fresh double cream
For the sides:
a few almonds, blanched, thinly sliced and browned

For the filling, blend the gelatine with the water and leave to swell for 10 minutes. Blend the pudding powder and the sugar with 4 tbsp. of the 1/2 pt. water; bring the rest of the water to the boil. Remove from heat and stir in the blended blancmange powder slowly; return to heat and allow to boil up again. Remove from the heat and stir in the gelatine mixture, continuing to stir until all is dissolved. Stir in the wine and the lemon juice and set aside to cool.

Whip the cream and when the pudding mixture begins to set but is not yet firm, fold the cream into it.

Cut the cake through once horizontally and spread the bottom half with 3/4 of the filling. Lay the other half on top and press well. Coat the top and sides evenly with some of the remaining filling and sprinkle the sides with almond slices. Pipe the rest of the filling as decoration on top of the cake.

Chocolate-Cream Sponge Cake

1 cake made with sponge mixture (1) see page 106
Icing:
3 1/2 oz. (100 g) icing sugar
2 level tbsp. cocoa
2 tbsp. hot water
3/4 oz. (20 g) coconut butter (melted)
Filling:
1 packet Oetker Regina Gelatine, ground white
4 tbsp. cold water for blending
1 3/4 pt. (750 ccm) fresh double cream
3 1/2 oz. (100 g) icing sugar
1 packet Oetker Vanillin Sugar
3 level tbsp. cocoa
For the sides:
3/4 oz. (20 g) chocolate (grated)

Cut the cake through once horizontally.
For the icing, sieve the cocoa and the icing sugar and blend with as much of the water as will give a good coating consistency; add the hot fat. Coat the top of the cake evenly with the icing.
For the filling, blend the gelatine with water, leave for 10 minutes to swell, then warm carefully until the gelatine is melted. Leave to cool. Whip the cream until almost stiff, then whisk in the lukewarm gelatine solution, the sieved icing sugar and the vanillin sugar. Whip the cream till quite stiff and fill 3 tbsp. of it into a forcing bag. Mix the sieved cocoa into the rest of the cream. Spread a good 2/3 of this cream onto the bottom layer of the cake. Cut the iced top of the cake into 12 equal pieces and place these carefully on the filling, and press lightly. Coat the sides of the cake with the rest of the brown cream. Pipe the white cream decoratively onto the top of the cake and sprinkle the sides with the grated chocolate.

Butter Cream-filled Cake (Phot. page 109)

1 cake made with sponge mixture (2) or (3) see page 106

Butter cream filling:
1 packet Oetker Pudding Powder, vanilla, almond, cream, caramel, or lemon flavour
3½ oz. (100 g) sugar
almost 1 pt. (570 ccm) cold milk
9 oz. (250 g) butter or margarine

Jam filling:
2–3 tbsp. jam

For the sides:
a few almonds (blanched and finely sliced)

or

Chocolate butter cream filling:
1 packet Oetker Pudding Powder, chocolate flavour
or 1 packet Oetker Gala Chocolate Pudding Powder
or 1 packet Oetker Pudding Powder, vanilla flavour and 2 level tbsp. cocoa
3½ oz. (100 g) sugar
almost 1 pt. (570 ccm) cold milk
9 oz. (250 g) butter or margarine

For the sides:
a few almonds (blanched and sliced) or chocolate vermicelli

or

Mocca butter cream filling:
1 packet Oetker Pudding Powder, cream flavour
3½–5½ oz. (100–150 g) sugar
almost 1 pt. (570 ccm) cold milk
2 tsp. instant coffee powder
9 oz. (250 g) butter or margarine

For the sides:
chocolate vermicelli
For mocca chocolate butter cream use 1 packet Oetker Gala Chocolate Pudding Powder instead of the one with the cream flavour

For the butter cream, blend the pudding powder and the sugar (and cocoa if mentioned in recipe) with 6 tbsp. of the milk. Bring the rest of the milk to the boil. Remove from heat and slowly stir in the blended pudding powder; boil up once more and stir in the instant coffee powder if mentioned in the recipe. Stir the pudding now and again while it cools. Cream the fat and beat in the cooled pudding a tbsp. at a time (neither fat nor pudding should be too cool otherwise the cream may curdle).

Cut the cake through twice horizontally. Spread the bottom layer with first either a thin layer of jam and then a good ¼ of the butter cream filling, or else only with a good ¼ of the cream, according to the recipe. Lay the 2nd layer over the filling, spread with a little less than half the remaining cream and lay the top layer over it. Coat the sides and the top surface thinly and evenly with a little of the remaining cream and sprinkle the sides with almonds or chocolate vermicelli. Pipe the rest of the cream decoratively over the top.

Pineapple-Cream Cake

1 cake made with sponge mixture (1) see page 106
Filling:
1 tin pineapples (8 slices)
1/2 pt. (285 ccm) pineapple juice
2 slightly heaped tbsp. Gustin (corn starch powder)
1 well heaped tbsp. sugar
3 slightly heaped tsp. Oetker Regina Gelatine, ground white
3 tbsp. cold water for blending
1 pt. (570 ccm) fresh double cream
1 3/4–2 1/2 oz. (50–75 g) icing sugar
1/2 level tsp. Oetker Regina Gelatine, ground white

For the filling, drain the pineapple slices in a sieve and then cut 5 slices into small pieces and 3 slices into quarters. Take away 1 tbsp. from the juice and measure off 1/2 pt. (if necessary make up the amount with water). Blend the Gustin and the sugar with 4 tbsp. of the juice and bring the rest to the boil; remove from heat and slowly stir in the blended Gustin; allow to boil up once more. Mix in the small pieces of pineapple and set aside to cool. Blend the 2 slightly heaped tsp. gelatine with the water and leave for ten minutes to swell; then warm carefully, stirring all the time until the gelatine is dissolved; set aside to cool. Whip the cream until almost stiff, then whisk in the lukewarm gelatine and the sieved icing sugar. Whip the cream till quite stiff and fold half of it into the cold juice jelly. Cut the cake through once horizontally and spread the bottom half with pineapple cream filling. Cut the upper half into 12 equal segments and lay these carefully on the cream, pressing lightly into place. Spread the sides and top of the cake evenly with more of the remaining cream. Lay a quarter slice of pineapple on each piece of cake and decorate with the rest of the cream.
Blend the 1/2 tsp. gelatine with the left over 1 tbsp. juice; leave for ten minutes to swell, then warm carefully, stirring all the time until the gelatine is completely dissolved. Brush the pieces of pineapple on the cake with this glaze.

Cottage Cheese Cream Cake (Phot. page 53)

1 cake made with sponge mixture (1) see page 106
Filling:
9 oz. (250 g) cottage cheese
2–4 tbsp. milk
3 1/2 oz. (100 g) sugar
a little grated lemon rind
juice of half a lemon
1 packet Oetker Regina Gelatine, ground white
2 tbsp. cold water for blending
1/2 pt. (285 ccm) fresh double cream
1 packet Oetker Vanillin Sugar

For the filling, rub the cottage cheese through a fine sieve and mix with enough milk to give a creamy consistency; then add the sugar, the lemon rind and the juice. Blend the gelatine with the water and leave ten minutes to swell; then warm carefully, stirring all the time, until the gelatine is quite dissolved. Cool until lukewarm, then stir into the cottage cheese mixture.
Whip the cream until thick, sweeten with the vanillin sugar and fold carefully into the cottage cheese mixture. Cut the cake through once horizontally and spread a good half of the filling on the bottom half. Lay the top half on the filling and spread the sides and top evenly with more filling. Pipe the rest of the cottage cheese cream filling decoratively over the top.

Orange Tart   Recipe page 119

Strawberry Cream Cake (Phot. page 89)

1 cake made with sponge mixture (1) see page 106
Filling:
1 packet Oetker Sauce Powder, vanilla flavour
1 well heaped tbsp. sugar
a little less than ½ pt. (285 ccm) cold milk
1⅛ lb. (500 g) strawberries
2 slightly heaped tsp. Oetker Regina Gelatine, ground white
3 tbsp. cold water for blending
¾ pt. (425 ccm) and 5 tbsp. fresh double cream
2 well heaped tbsp. icing sugar
1 packet Oetker Vanillin Sugar

For the filling, blend the milk gradually with the sauce powder and sugar and bring to the boil, stirring all the time; allow to boil up briefly. Set aside to cool, stirring now and again to prevent a skin forming.

Wash the strawberries, drain well and pick them over. Blend the gelatine with the water and leave to swell for ten minutes. Warm carefully, stirring all the time until the gelatine is quite dissolved, then cool.

Whip the cream until almost thick, then add the lukewarm gelatine solution, sieved icing sugar and vanillin sugar. Whip the cream until completely thick.

Cut the cake through once horizontally and spread the bottom with cold blancmange; distribute the strawberries over it and spread about ¾ of the cream over them. Cut the top of the cake into 12 equal pieces and lay these on the cream, pressing lightly into place. Coat the sides and the top of the cake with some of the remaining cream and pipe the rest on the top as decoration.

Truffle Cake

1 cake made with sponge mixture (4) see page 106
Filling:
4½ oz. (125 g) butter
5½ oz. (150 g) icing sugar
3½ oz. (100 g) cocoa
1 egg
1 bottle Oetker rum flavour
2 tbsp. water
1 packet Oetker Vanillin Sugar
Icing:
5½ oz. (150 g) icing sugar
3 level tbsp. cocoa
2–3 tbsp. hot water
if desired ¾ oz. (20 g) coconut butter (melted)
For the sides:
2½ oz. (70 g) chocolate vermicelli

For the filling, sieve together the cocoa and the icing sugar. Cream the butter and gradually add some of the cocoa and icing sugar; mix in the egg, then add the rest of the icing sugar and cocoa; stir in the rum flavour. Take away from the filling 16 tsp.; each tsp. should contain so much that a ball as big as a cherry can be formed from it; put aside to cool well through. Mix the water and the vanillin sugar into the rest. Cut the cake through twice and fill with the chocolate filling.

For the icing, sieve together the cocoa and the icing sugar and blend with as much water as will give a good coating consistency; add the hot fat, then ice the cake with it – top and sides. Coat the sides with chocolate vermicelli and sprinkle around the edge of the top in a 1 in. (2 cm) border. Form little balls out of the filling which was put aside to cool, roll these in chocolate vermicelli and lay them in a ring on top of the cake.

Black Forest Cherry Cake

Pastry:
4½ oz. (125 g) plain flour
1 level tbsp. cocoa
1 level tsp. (3 g) Oetker Baking Powder Backin
2 well heaped tbsp. sugar
1 packet Oetker Vanillin Sugar
1 egg white
1¾ oz. (50 g) butter or margarine

Sponge mixture:
4 egg yolks
2 tbsp. warm water
3½ oz. (100 g) sugar
1 packet Oetker Vanillin Sugar
3 drops Oetker Baking Essence, bitter almond flavour
a good pinch cinnamon
3 egg whites
2½ oz. (75 g) plain flour
1 level tbsp. cocoa
3 slightly heaped tbsp. Oetker Gustin (corn starch powder)
½ level tsp. (3 g) Oetker Baking Powder Backin

Filling:
1¾ lb. (750 g) morello cherries
2½–3½ oz. (75–100 g) sugar
4 slightly heaped tbsp. Oetker Gustin (corn starch powder)
2 tbsp. Schwarzwälder Kirschwasser (cherry spirits)
2 slightly heaped tsp. Oetker Regina Gelatine, ground white
3 tbsp. cold water for blending
¾ pt. (425 ccm) fresh double cream
1 packet Oetker Vanillin Sugar
1 tbsp. icing sugar

For sprinkling:
1 oz. (30 g) grated chocolate

For the pastry, mix and sieve together the flour, cocoa and the Backin onto a pastry board or cool slab. Make a well in the centre and pour in the sugar, vanillin sugar and the egg white. Draw some of the flour from the sides of the well to mix with these to form a thickish paste. Add the cold fat, cut into small pieces, cover the whole with more of the flour and, starting from the middle, work all these ingredients quickly with the hands into a smooth firm paste. If it should stick, cool well through for some time. Grease the base of a round cake tin, diameter 10 in. (26 cm) and roll out the pastry to fit it.

Oven: pre-heat for 5 minutes at very hot, bake at moderately hot.

Baking time: about 20 minutes.

For the sponge mixture, whisk the egg yolks with the water until frothy, then add ⅔ of the sugar with the vanillin sugar, a little at a time. Continue whisking until the mixture is thick and creamy; add the flavourings and cinnamon. Whisk the egg whites in a separate bowl until stiff enough to show and retain the cut of a knife; gradually whisk in the rest of the sugar. Fill the egg white snow onto the egg yolk mixture. Mix together the flour, Gustin, cocoa, and Backin and sieve onto the egg whites. Fold all gently together (do not stir or beat). Line a round cake tin, the same size as the one used for the pastry base, with paper. Fill the sponge mixture into it and bake immediately.

Oven: moderately hot.

Baking time: 30–35 minutes.

For the filling, wash and stone the cherries. Mix with 2½ oz. (75 g) sugar and leave for a short time to allow juice to collect. Then bring to the boil and drain in a sieve or colander, collecting the juice below. When cherries and juice are cold, measure off ½ pt. juice (if necessary make up the amount with water) and blend 4 tbsp. of it with the Gustin. Bring the rest of the juice to the boil, remove from heat, stir in the prepared Gustin; return to heat nad boil up briefly. Mix in the cherries and put aside to cool; when cold sweeten to taste with the rest of the sugar and the Schwarzwälder Kirschwasser. Blend the gelatine with the water and set aside for ten minutes to swell; stir over a low heat until the gelatine is completely dissolved, then cool. Whip the cream until almost thick, then add the lukewarm gela-

Continuation s. page 120

tine solution, the vanillin sugar, and the icing sugar; continue whisking until quite stiff. Spread half of the cherry mixture and $1/3$ of the cream over the pastry base. Cut the sponge through once horizontally and lay one half on the pastry base, pressing well. Cover with the rest of the cherry filling and half of the remaining cream. Cover this with the other sponge half and pile the rest of the cream on the top. Sprinkle with the grated chocolate and cool well through before cutting.

Coffee Cream Cake

1 cake made with sponge mixture (1) see page 106
Filling:
1 packet Oetker Regina Gelatine, ground white
4 tbsp. cold water for blending
$1^{1}/_{3}$ pt. (750 ccm) fresh double cream
$3^{1}/_{2}$ oz. (100 g) icing sugar
1 packet Oetker Vanillin Sugar
2 tsp. instant coffee powder
For the sides:
chocolate vermicelli
For decorating:
12 chocolate coffee-beans

For the filling, blend the gelatine with the water and leave to swell for ten minutes. Warm carefully, stirring all the time until the gelatine is completely dissolved, then set aside to cool.
Whisk the cream until almost thick; mix in the lukewarm gelatine, the sieved icing sugar and the vanillin sugar. Whisk the cream until quite thick, then mix in the instant coffee powder.
Cut the cake through once horizontally and spread the bottom with $2/3$ of the coffee cream. Cut the top into 12 equal parts and lay these carefully on the filling, pressing lightly into place. Coat the sides and the top evenly with some of the remaining cream, sprinkle the sides with chocolate vermicelli and pipe the rest of the cream over the top of the cake, decorating with the chocolate coffee-beans.

Sacher Cake

Sponge mixture:
6 egg yolks
2 tbsp. warm water
6 oz. (170 g) sugar
1 packet Oetker Vanillin Sugar
6 egg whites
3½ oz. (100 g) plain flour
2 packets Oetker Gala Chocolate Blancmange Powder
5 level tbsp. cocoa
2 level tsp. (6 kg) Oetker Baking Powder Backin
5½ oz. (150 g) butter or margarine (melted)
For filling and coating:
about 5½ oz. (150 g) apricot jam
Icing:
5½ oz. (150 g) icing sugar
3 level tbsp. cocoa
about 3 tbsp. hot water
1¼ oz. (40 g) coconut butter (melted)
For decorating:
2½ oz. (70 g) almonds (blanched and finely chopped)

For the sponge mixture, whisk the egg yolks with the water until frothy, then add ⅔ of the sugar with the vanillin sugar, a little at a time. Continue whisking until the mixture is thick and creamy. Whisk the egg whites in a separate bowl until stiff enough to show and retain the cut of a knife; gradually whisk in the rest of the sugar. Fill the egg white snow onto the egg yolk mixture. Mix together the flour, the blancmange powder, the cocoa and the Backin and sieve onto the egg whites. Fold all gently together (do not stir or beat) at the same time adding gradually the cooled fat. Line a round cake tin with a removable rim, diameter 10 in. (26 cm) with paper and fill the cake mixture into it, baking immediately.
Oven: moderately hot.
Baking time: 35–45 minutes.
Fill and ice the cake the following day.
Cut the cake through horizontally once, fill with apricot jam and coat the sides and top thinly and evenly with the jam.
For the icing, sieve the cocoa and the icing sugar and blend with as much water as will give a good coating consistency; add the hot fat and coat the cake with the icing. Sprinkle the sides and a border of ¾ in. (about 2 cm) round the outer edge of the top with the almonds.

Zuger Kirsch Cake

Sponge mixture:
4 egg yolks
2–3 tbsp. warm water*
3½ oz. (100 g) sugar
1 packet Oetker Vanillin Sugar
1 egg white
2½ oz. (75 g) plain flour
5 slightly heaped tbsp. Oetker Gustin (corn starch powder)
1 level tsp. (3 g) Oetker Baking Powder Backin

* If the eggs are rather large, take the smaller quantity of water; if they are small, take the larger.

For the sponge mixture, whisk the egg yolks with the water until frothy, then add ⅔ of the sugar and the vanillin sugar, a little at a time. Continue whisking until the mixture is thick and creamy. Whisk the egg white in a separate bowl until stiff enough to show and retain the cut of a knife; gradually whisk in the rest of the sugar. Fill the egg white snow onto the egg yolk mixture. Mix together the flour, the Gustin and the Backin and sieve onto the egg white. Fold all gently together (do not stir or beat). Line a round cake tin with a removable rim, diameter 10 in. (26 cm) with paper, fill in the cake mixture and bake immediately.
Oven: moderately hot.
Baking time: 25–30 minutes.
Continuation s. page 122

Meringue layers:
3 egg whites
5½ oz. (150 g) castor sugar
1 packet Oetker Vanillin Sugar
3½ oz. (100 g) ground almonds

Filling:
1 packet Oetker Pudding Powder, raspberry flavour
3½ oz. (100 g) sugar
6 tbsp. cold milk for blending
almost 1 pt. (570 ccm) milk
9 oz. (250 g) butter or margarine

To moisten the cake:
6 tbsp. water
3 slightly heaped tbsp. sugar
6 tbsp. Schwarzwälder Kirschwasser (cherry spirits)

For decorating the sides:
1¾ oz. (50 g) almonds (blanched)

For dusting:
1 well heaped tbsp. icing sugar

For the meringue layers, whisk the egg whites until stiff; the snow must be firm enough to show and retain the cut of a knife. Gradually whisk in the rest of the sugar and the vanillin sugar and carefully fold in the almonds. Grease a round cake tin and line with well greased paper. Fill into it half of the meringue mixture and smooth it evenly.

Oven: slow.

Baking time: about 90 minutes.

As soon as the meringue is baked, brush the paper with water and remove it. Bake the second meringue layer in the same way. If the cake is to be made the following day store the meringue layers in an airtight tin (large pan) so that they will not soften.

For the filling, blend the pudding powder and the sugar with the milk. Bring the ½ pt. milk to the boil; remove from heat; stir in the blended pudding powder; return to heat and allow to boil up once. Set aside to cool, stirring now and again to prevent a skin forming. Cream the fat and add the cooled blancmange, a tablespoon at a time (take care that neither fat nor pudding are too cold otherwise the cream may curdle).

To moisten the cake, boil up the sugar and water and cool. Then add the Kirschwasser. Spread ¼ of the butter cream over one of the meringue layers, place on this the sponge layer, sprinkle with the cold Kirschwasser, then spread with almost half the rest of the butter cream; lay the second meringue layer on this and coat the top and sides of the cake evenly with the rest of the cream.

For the sides, chop the almonds very finely and roast them lightly on a baking sheet in the oven until golden, turning them over now and again. Leave to cool, then coat the sides of the cake with them. Draw a knife blade, dipped in hot water, over the top of the cake to give a trellis pattern. Sieve the icing sugar evenly over the top. The cake tastes best and is easier to cut, if eaten the following day.

Nut Cream Cake and Fruit Salad Flan

Sponge mixture for both cakes:
4 egg yolks
4–5 tbsp. warm water*
7 oz. (200 g) sugar
1 packet Oetker Vanillin Sugar
4 egg whites
4½ oz. (125 g) plain flour
4½ oz. (125 g) Oetker Gustin (corn starch powder)
3 level tsp. (9 g) Oetker Baking Powder Backin

Filling for the nut cream cake:
5½ oz. (150 g) hazelnuts (ground)
2 slightly heaped tsp. Oetker Regina Gelatine, ground white
3 tbsp. cold water for blending
¾ pt. (425 ccm) and 5 tbsp. fresh double cream
1 well heaped tbsp. icing sugar
1 packet Oetker Vanillin Sugar

For decorating:
12–16 hazelnuts

Topping for the fruit salad flan:
1 packet Oetker Sauce Powder, vanilla flavour
1 well heaped tbsp. sugar
almost ½ pt. (285 ccm) cold milk
2 apples, 2 bananas, 2 oranges
1 well heaped tbsp. sugar
1 packet Oetker Vanillin Sugar

Glaze:
1 packet Oetker Cake Glaze, transparent
½ pt. (285 ccm) water or fruit juice
sugar according to instructions on the glaze packet

* If the eggs are rather large, take the smaller quantity of water; if they are small, take the larger.

For the sponge mixture, whisk the yolks with the water until frothy, then add ⅔ of the sugar, and the vanillin sugar, a little at a time. Continue whisking until the mixture is thick and creamy. Whisk the egg whites in a separate bowl until stiff enough to show and retain the cut of a knife; gradually whisk in the rest of the sugar. Fill the egg white snow onto the whisked egg yolk mixture. Mix together the flour, Gustin and Backin and sieve onto the egg whites. Fold all gently together – do not stir or beat. Line a round cake tin with a removable rim, diameter 10 in. (26 cm) with paper; fill the cake mixture into it and bake immediately.
Oven: moderately hot.
Baking time: 20–30 minutes.
When cool, cut the cake horizontally into three pieces. Use the top layer for the Fruit Salad Flan and the other two for the Nut Cream Cake.
For the nut cream cake, brown the hazelnuts in a pan, then leave to cool. Blend the gelatine with the water and leave for ten minutes to swell. Warm carefully over a slow heat, stirring all the time until the gelatine is completely dissolved, then set aside to cool.
Whip the cream until almost thick, then whisk in the lukewarm gelatine mixture, the sieved icing sugar and the vanillin sugar. Continue whisking until the cream is quite thick. Fill ⅔ of the cream into a piping bag and mix the cooled nuts (take away 2 tbsp. first) into the rest of the cream.
Spread the bottom layer of the sponge with the nut cream filling, lay the next layer on top and coat the top and sides evenly with some of the cream from the piping bag. Coat the sides of the cake with the 2 tbsp. ground nuts. Pipe about half the remaining cream on top of the cake and decorate with the whole hazelnuts.
For the fruit salad flan, blend the sauce powder and the sugar gradually with the milk and bring to the boil; boil up briefly. Set aside to cool, stirring now and again, then spread over the cut surface of the remaining cake layer. Peel the fruit and cut up as small as possible, mixing carefully with the sugar and the vanillin sugar. Distribute the fruit salad evenly over the remaining sponge layer. Prepare the glaze according to the directions on the packet and pour over the fruit. Decorate with the rest of the cream in the forcing bag.

Fruit Flan

Sponge mixture:
1 egg, 3 tbsp. warm water
2½ oz. (75 g) sugar
1 packet Oetker Vanillin Sugar
3½ oz. (100 g) plain flour
1 level tsp. (3 g) Oetker Baking Powder Backin

Custard and fruit topping:
1 packet Oetker Sauce Powder, vanilla flavour
1 well heaped tbsp. sugar
almost ½ pt. (285 ccm) cold milk
1⅛–1¾ lb. (500–750 g) fruit
 (raw, stewed, tinned or bottled)
(e.g. pineapples, apples, apricots, strawberries, cherries, peaches, gooseberries, etc.)

Glaze:
1 packet Oetker Cake Glaze, transparent
½ pt. (285 ccm) water or fruit juice
sugar according to the instructions on the glaze packet

For decorating:
a few almonds (blanched and sliced) or hazelnuts (sliced)

For the sponge mixture, whisk the egg and water until frothy, then gradually add the sugar and the vanillin sugar. Continue whisking until the mixture is thick and creamy. Mix together the flour and the Backin and sieve onto the whisked egg mixture. Fold all gently together – do not stir or beat. Grease a round cake tin with a removable rim, diameter 10 in. (26 cm) and line with paper. Fill the sponge mixture into it and bake immediately.

Oven: moderately hot. **Baking time:** 20–25 minutes.

For the topping, blend the sauce powder and the sugar gradually with the milk; bring to the boil stirring all the time and allow to boil up briefly. Stir it now and again during cooling and when cool, spread over the inside of the flan case.

Soft fruits may be used raw and should be prepared as follows: apricots, strawberries and peaches should be washed and well drained, stoned or picked over according to kind.

Stewed fruit (peel apples, cut into quarters or eighths and poach carefully in syrup) or bottled or tinned fruit should be well drained. Lay the prepared fruits on the flan case. Prepare the glaze according to the instructions on the packet, pour over the fruit and decorate the sides with the sliced nuts.

Orange Butter Cream Cake

1 cake made with sponge mixture (2) see page 106

Filling:
1 packet Oetker Fruttina Pudding Powder, lemon flavour
3 slightly heaped tbsp. Gustin (corn starch powder)
5½ oz. (150 g) sugar
almost ¼ pt. (140 ccm) orange juice (pressed from 2 large or 3 small oranges)
⅔ pt. (375 ccm) water
9 oz. (250 g) butter or margarine

For the sides:
a few almonds (blanched and sliced)

For decorating:
12–16 orange segments

For the filling, blend together the blancmange powder, Gustin and sugar with the orange juice; bring the water to the boil, remove from heat, stir in the blended ingredients slowly and boil up again. Stir now and again as it cools.

Cream the fat and beat in the cooled pudding a tablespoon at a time (neither the fat nor the blancmange should be too cool otherwise the butter cream may curdle).

Cut the cake through twice horizontally and spread the bottom layer with a good ¼ of the cream, lay the middle layer on this and spread with almost ½ the remaining cream, lay the top of the cake on this. Coat the top and sides thinly and evenly with more cream and coat the sides with almonds. Lay the orange segments in a pattern on the top and pipe the rest of the cream as decoration over the top.

Orange Tart (Phot. page 110)

Sponge mixture:
3 egg yolks
2–3 tbsp. warm water*
4½ oz. (125 g) sugar
1 packet Oetker Vanillin Sugar
3 egg whites
2½ oz. (70 g) plain flour
2½ oz. (70 g) Oetker Gustin
  (corn starch powder)
2 level tsp. (6 g) Oetker Baking
  Powder Backin
2 level tbsp. cocoa
Filling:
1 packet Oetker Regina Gelatine,
  ground white
2 tbsp. cold water for blending
6 tbsp. orange juice, a little grated
  rind of orange, almost 2 tbsp.
  orange marmalade
1⅓ pt. (750 ccm) fresh double cream
1¾ oz. (50 g) icing sugar
For decorating:
12–16 orange segments

*If the eggs are rather large, take the smaller quantity of water; if they are small, take the larger.

For the sponge mixture, whisk the egg yolks with the water until frothy, then add ⅔ of the sugar and the vanillin sugar, a little at a time; continue whisking until the mixture is thick and creamy. Whisk the egg whites in a separate bowl until stiff enough to show and retain the cut of a knife, then gradually whisk in the rest of the sugar. Fill the egg white snow onto the whisked egg yolk mixture. Mix together the flour, Gustin, Backin and cocoa and sieve onto the egg whites. Fold all the ingredients gently together (do not stir or beat). Line the base of a round cake tin with a removable rim, diameter 10 in. (26 cm) with paper and fill into it the sponge mixture. Bake immediately.
Oven: moderately hot.
Baking time: 20–30 minutes.
Cool the cake well through.
For the filling, blend the gelatine with water, leave for 10 minutes to swell, then warm carefully until the gelatine is melted. Add the orange juice and the grated rind. Leave to cool. Whip the cream until almost stiff, then whisk in the lukewarm gelatine solution and the sieved icing sugar. Whip the cream till quite stiff.
Cut the cake through twice horizontally. Spread the bottom layer with a thin layer of jam and then a good ⅓ of the filling. Lay the 2nd layer over the filling, spread with a little less than half the remaining cream and lay the top layer over it. Coat the sides and the top surface thinly and evenly with a little of the remaining cream. Pipe the rest of the cream as decoration over the top and arrange the orange segments in a pattern on the top.

Kaiser's Cake

Pastry:
9 oz. (250 g) plain flour
1 level tsp. (3 g) Oetker Baking
  Powder Backin
2½ oz. (75 g) sugar
1 packet Oetker Vanillin Sugar
2 tbsp. milk or water
4½ oz. (125 g) butter or margarine

For the pastry, mix and sieve together the flour and the Backin onto a pastry board or cool slab. Make a well in the centre and pour in the sugar, the vanillin sugar and the liquid. Draw in some of the flour from the sides of the well to mix with these to form a thickish paste. Add the cold fat, cut into small pieces and cover the whole with more of the flour. Starting from the middle, work all these ingredients quickly with the hands into a smooth firm paste. If it should stick, coll well through for some time.

Continuation s. page 126

Sponge mixture:
6 egg yolks
7 oz. (200 g) sugar
1 packet Oetker Vanillin Sugar
1 bottle Oetker rum flavour
6 egg whites
9 oz. (250 g) plain flour
1 level tsp. (3 g) Oetker Baking Powder Backin
$3^1/2$ oz. (100 g) almonds (blanched and chopped)
$5^1/2$–7 oz. (150–200 g) sultanas (washed and well drained)
$3^1/2$ oz. (100 g) candied lemon peel (diced)
$4^1/2$ oz. (125 g) butter or margarine (melted)

Roll out $1/3$ of the pastry to fit the base of a round cake tin with a removable rim, diameter 10 in. (26 cm). Using half the remaining pastry, roll out a round as large as the cake tin and cut with a pastry wheel into 16–20 equal strips. Form the rest of the pastry into a roll, lay this around the inner edge of the cake form, then press up against the rim so that the cake sides are 1 in. (3 cm) high.

For the sponge mixture, whisk the egg yolk, then add gradually $2/3$ of the sugar and the vanillin sugar; continue whisking until the mixture is thick and creamy, then add the baking essence. Whisk the egg whites in a separate bowl until stiff enough to show and retain the cut of a knife; gradually whisk in the rest of the sugar. Fill the egg white snow onto the egg yolk mixture. Mix together the flour and the Backin and sieve onto the egg whites; sprinkle over this the almonds, sultanas and candied lemon peel. Fold all the ingredients gently together, at the same time adding the cooled fat gradually. Fill the sponge mixture into the pastry case, smooth it evenly and lay the pastry strips in a trellis pattern on top.

Oven: moderately hot.
Baking time: 65–80 minutes.

MAKING A SPONGE ROLL

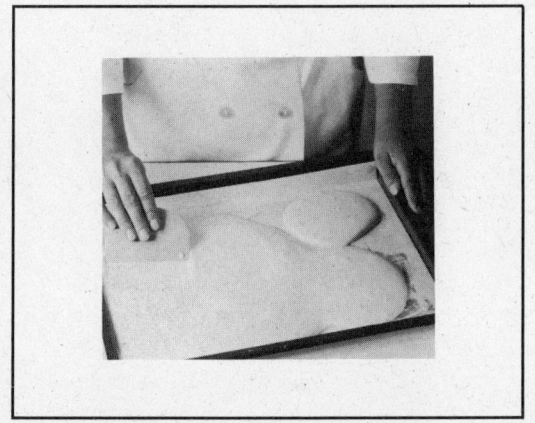

FIVE SIMPLE STEPS

1. The baking sheet should be lined with greaseproof paper. To do this, grease the baking sheet in about three places – if possible with a brush – then lay the paper on the sheet, pressing well against it and fold the paper on the open side a few times so that an edge is formed and the cake mixture cannot run off. Spread the sponge mixture evenly over the sheet about 1/2 in. (1 cm) thick.

2. After baking remove from oven and loosen the sponge at once from the sides of the baking sheet and from the paper edge with a knife. With the help of the paper underneath sticking to the sponge, lift it from the baking sheet and turn onto a paper sprinkled with sugar.

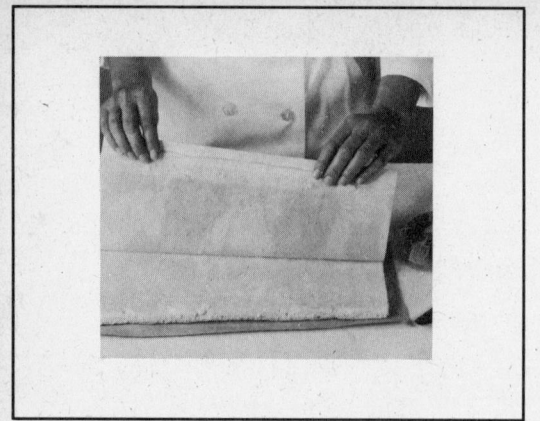

3. Brush the greaseproof paper sticking to the sponge with cold water and, working carefully and quickly, peel off the paper.

4. Quickly spread the sponge with jam.

5. Roll up the sponge, starting at the shorter side.

CAKES ON A BAKING SHEET

Sponge Mixture for Rolls and Slices

Sponge mixture (1):
3 egg yolks
5–6 tbsp. warm water*
5½ oz. (150 g) sugar
1 packet Oetker Vanillin Sugar
3 egg whites
3½ oz. (100 g) plain flour
5 slightly heaped tbsp. Oetker Gustin (corn starch powder)
1 level tsp. (3 g) Oetker Baking Powder Backin

Sponge mixture (2):
4 egg yolks
3–4 tbsp. warm water*
4½ oz. (125 g) sugar
1 packet Oetker Vanillin Sugar
4 egg whites
2½ oz. (75 g) plain flour
5 slightly heaped tbsp. Oetker Gustin (corn starch powder)
a pinch of Oetker Baking Powder Backin

Sponge mixture (3):
4 egg yolks
4 tbsp. warm water
4½ oz. (125 g) sugar
1 packet Oetker Vanillin Sugar
4 egg whites
5 level tbsp. plain flour
5 slightly heaped tbsp. Oetker Gustin (corn starch powder)
3 level tbsp. cocoa
½ level tsp. (1½ g) Oetker Baking Powder Backin

* If the eggs are rather large, take the smaller quantity of water; if they are small, take the larger.

For the sponge mixture, whisk the egg yolks with the water until frothy, then add ⅔ of the sugar and the vanillin sugar, a little at a time. Continue whisking until the mixture is thick and creamy. Whisk the egg whites in a separate bowl until stiff enough to show and retain the cut of a knife; gradually whisk in the rest of the sugar. Fill the egg white snow onto the egg yolk mixture. Mix together the flour, Gustin and Backin (and cocoa for sponge mixture 3) and sieve onto the egg whites. Fold all gently together (do not stir or beat). Line a baking sheet with greaseproof paper and spread the cake mixture over this about ½ in. (1 cm) thick. Crease the paper together a few times at the open end of the baking sheet to form an edge so that the mixture cannot run off.
Oven: pre-heat for 5 minutes at very hot, bake at very hot.
Baking time: 10–15 minutes.

Chocolate Sponge Roll

Sponge roll mixture (3) see page 123
Filling:
1 packet Oetker Pudding Powder,
   vanilla flavour
3½ oz. (100 g) sugar
¾ pt. (425 ccm) and 5 tbsp. cold milk
7 oz. (200 g) butter or margarine

After baking the sponge, turn it right away onto a paper sprinkled with sugar. Brush the greaseproof paper with cold water, then peel the paper quickly and carefully off the sponge. Roll up with the underneath paper and leave to cool.
For the filling, blend the pudding powder and the sugar with the 5 tbsp. milk. Bring the ¾ pt. milk to the boil; remove from heat; stir in the prepared pudding powder mixture slowly; return to heat and boil up briefly. Set aside to cool stirring now and again. Cream the fat and add the cooled pudding, a tablespoon at a time (take care that neither fat nor pudding are too cold, otherwise the cream may curdle).
Unroll the cooled roll very carefully and spread almost half of the butter cream evenly over it; roll up again. Coat the roll with some of the remaining cream and pipe the rest onto it as decoration.

Wine-Cream Roll

Sponge roll mixture (2) see page 123
Filling:
1 packet Oetker Regina Gelatine,
   ground white
2 tbsp. cold water for blending
1 packet Oetker Fruttina Pudding
   Powder, lemon flavour
4½ oz. (125 g) sugar
½ pt. (¼ l) water (285 ccm)
½ pt. (¼ l) hock or similar white wine
   (285 ccm)
1 tbsp. lemon juice (if desired)
¼–½ pt. (⅛–¼ l) fresh double cream
   (140–285 ccm)
For decorating:
1¾ oz. (50 g) almonds
   (blanched and sliced)

After baking the sponge, turn it right away onto a paper sprinkled with sugar. Brush the greaseproof paper with cold water, then peel the paper quickly but carefully off the sponge. Roll up with the underneath paper and leave to cool.
Prepare the almond slices for decorating by roasting lightly on a baking sheet in a moderate oven until golden brown, then cool.
For the filling, blend the gelatine with the water and leave for ten minutes to swell.
Blend the pudding powder and sugar with 4 tbsp. of the ½ pt. (¼ l) water. Bring the rest of the water to the boil; remove from heat; stir in the prepared Fruttina powder gradually and boil up briefly. Remove from heat and stir in the soaked gelatine; stir until quite dissolved. Finally stir in the wine and the lemon juice and set aside to cool. As soon as it begins to thicken fold in the whipped cream.
Unroll the cooled sponge very carefully and spread evenly with the wine-cream filling (leave a little for decorating the outside). Roll up again, then coat with the rest of the cream and sprinkle with the sliced almonds.

Black Forest Roll

Sponge mixture:
4 egg yolks
3–4 tbsp. warm water
4 1/2 oz. (125 g) sugar
1 packet Oetker Vanillin Sugar
4 egg whites
2 1/2 oz. (75 g) plain flour
5 slightly heaped tbsp. Oetker Gustin (corn starch powder)
a good pinch of Oetker Baking Powder Backin
Filling:
1 packet Oetker Regina Gelatine, ground white
3 tbsp. cold water for blending
1 pt. (570 ccm) fresh double cream
1 1/4 oz. (40 g) sugar
1 packet Oetker Vanillin Sugar
2 tbsp. Kirschwasser (cherry spirits)
For coating:
about 3 1/2 oz. (100 g) grated bitter chocolate
For decorating:
a few candied cherries

For the sponge mixture, whisk the egg yolks with the water until frothy, then add 2/3 of the sugar, a little at a time; and the vanillin sugar. Continue whisking until the mixture is thick and creamy. Whisk the egg whites until stiff enough to show and retain the cut of a knife, then gradually whisk in the rest of the sugar. Fill the egg white snow onto the whisked egg yolk mixture. Mix together the flour, Gustin and Backin and sieve onto the egg whites, fold all the ingredients gently together (do not stir or beat). Line a baking sheet with greaseproof paper and spread the sponge mixture evenly over it about 1 in. (1 cm) thick. Crease the paper at the open end of the baking sheet to from a rim to prevent the mixture running off.
Oven: pre-heat for 5 minutes at very hot, bake at very hot.
Baking time: 10–15 minutes.
As soon as it is taken from the oven turn the sponge onto a paper sprinkled with sugar. Brush the greaseproof paper with cold water and carefully but quickly peel off. Roll up the sponge with the underneath paper and leave to cool.
For the filling, mix the gelatine with the water and leave 10 minutes to swell. Heat carefully, stirring all the time until the gelatine is completely dissolved, then leave to cool. Whisk the cream until almost finished, then add the luke-warm gelatine. Finish whisking the cream, and add sugar, vanillin sugar and Kirschwasser.
Carefully unroll the cooled sponge roll and spread 2/3 of the cream evenly over it; roll up again removing the outer brown skin if desired. Coat the outside with cream and sprinkle with the grated chocolate. Decorate with the remaining cream and the cherries.

Sponge Slices

Sponge roll mixture (1) see page 123
Filling:
1 packet Oetker Pudding Powder, vanilla flavour
2 well heaped tbsp. sugar
3/4 pt. cold milk (425 ccm)
3 1/2 oz. (100 g) butter or margarine

A sponge intended for a roll but not soft enough because baked too long, can very well be used for sponge slices.
After baking the sponge, turn it right away onto a paper sprinkled with sugar. Brush the greaseproof paper with cold water and quickly but carefully peel the paper off the sponge.
Continuation s. page 134

For brushing:
2–3 tbsp. jam

For the filling, blend the pudding powder and the sugar with 6 tbsp. of the milk. Bring the rest of the milk to the boil; remove from heat; stir in the blended pudding powder mixture gradually and return to heat, boiling up briefly. Stir the pudding now and again during cooling.

Cut the sponge into two halves; spread one half with jam and half the cooled pudding, then lay the other half sponge on top. Cream the fat and beat in the pudding a tbsp. at a time (take care that neither fat nor pudding are too cool otherwise the cream may curdle).

Coat the top surface of the cake thinly with the butter cream. Cut the cake into slices $1^{1}/_{2} \times 3$ in. (about $4^{1}/_{2} \times 8^{1}/_{2}$ cm) and decorate each by piping butter cream on the top.

Alternatively, some of the slices may be coated with chocolate icing before decorating with butter cream. For the chocolate icing, sieve together $2^{1}/_{2}$ oz. (75 g) icing sugar and 1 heaped tsp. cocoa and blend with about 1 tbsp. hot water until a good coating consistency is obtained.

Chocolate Log (Bismarck Oak)

Sponge roll mixture (2) see page 123
Filling:
1 packet Oetker Gala Chocolate Pudding Powder
$3^{1}/_{2}$ oz. (100 g) sugar
$^{3}/_{4}$ pt. (425 ccm) and 5 tbsp. cold milk
6–7 oz. (170–200 g) butter or margarine

After baking the sponge, turn it right away onto a paper sprinkled with sugar. Brush the greaseproof paper with cold water and peel the paper quickly and carefully off the sponge. Roll up with the underneath paper and leave to cool.

For the filling, blend the pudding powder and sugar with the 5 tbsp. milk. Bring the $^{3}/_{4}$ pt. milk to the boil; remove from heat; slowly stir in the prepared pudding powder; return to heat and boil up briefly. Stir now and again while the pudding cools. Cream the fat and add the pudding a tablespoon at a time (take care that neither fat nor pudding are too cool, otherwise the cream may curdle).

Unroll the cooled roll very carefully and spread with the butter cream leaving a little aside for decorating later; roll up again. Coat the roll with the rest of the cream and draw a fork along the surface to make wavy lines similar to those on a tree trunk.

Cinnamon Stars Recipe page 158
Lemon Hearts Recipe page 159

Honey and Nut Roll

Sponge roll mixture (1) or (2)
see page 123
Filling (1):
7 oz. (200 g) hazelnuts (ground)
4½ oz. (120 g) honey
   (about 6 level tbsp.)
¼ pt. (⅛ l) fresh double cream
   (140 ccm)
½ bottle Oetker rum flavour
or
Filling (2):
9–13 oz. (250–375 g) jam
For decorating:
a little icing sugar
   or 1¾ oz. (50 g) almonds
      (blanched and sliced)
   or hazelnuts (sliced)

While the sponge mixture for the roll is baking, mix together for Filling (1) the hazelnuts, honey, cream and rum flavour to a good spreading consistency.
As soon as it is baked, turn the sponge onto a paper sprinkled with sugar; brush the baking paper with cold water, then quickly but carefully peel off. Spread the sponge evenly with the honey filling or the jam and roll up from the shorter side. Dust the roll with icing sugar or spread thinly with jam and sprinkle with almond slices.

Strawberry Roll

Sponge roll mixture (2) see page 123
Filling:
about 1¾ lb. (750 g) strawberries
1 packet Oetker Regina Gelatine,
   ground white
3 tbsp. cold water for blending
1 slightly heaped tsp. Oetker Regina
   Gelatine, ground red
2 tbsp. cold water
¾ pt. (425 ccm) fresh double cream
2½ oz. (75 g) icing sugar
1 packet Oetker Vanillin Sugar
For decorating:
about 14 strawberries

After baking the sponge, turn it right away onto a paper sprinkled with sugar. Brush the greaseproof paper with cold water and quickly but carefully peel the paper off the sponge. Roll up the sponge with the underneath paper and leave to cool.
For the filling, wash the strawberries, drain well, remove stalks, pick over and cut into pieces. Blend the white gelatine with the water and leave 10 minutes to swell; heat carefully, stirring all the time until the gelatine is completely dissolved, then cool. Whip the cream until almost thick; add the lukewarm gelatine solution; continue whipping until the cream is quite thick, then whisk in the sieved icing sugar and the vanillin sugar. Fill almost half the cream into a forcing bag. Melt the red gelatine according to the instructions above for the white and, when lukewarm add to the rest of the cream; fold in the strawberries. Carefully unroll the sponge and spread the strawberry filling evenly over it; roll up again. Coat the roll with some cream from the piping bag and pipe the rest of the cream onto the roll, decorating with the strawberries.

Spekulatius   Recipe page 152

Hazelnut Roll

Sponge roll mixture (2) see page 123
Filling:
2 well heaped tsp. Oetker Regina Gelatine, ground white
3 tbsp. cold water for blending
$2/3$ pt. ($3/8$ l) fresh double cream (375 ccm)
1–2 drops Oetker Baking Essence, bitter almond flavour
$1^{3}/_{4}$ oz. (50 g) icing sugar
1 packet Oetker Vanillin Sugar
$3^{1}/_{2}$ oz. (100 g) hazelnuts (ground and lightly roasted)
For decorating:
a few hazelnuts (sliced)

After baking the sponge, turn it right away onto a paper sprinkled with sugar. Brush the greaseproof paper with cold water, then peel the paper quickly but carefully off the sponge. Roll up with the underneath paper and leave to cool.

For the filling, blend the gelatine with the water and leave for ten minutes to swell; then heat carefully, stirring all the time, until the gelatine is quite dissolved. Whip the cream until almost thick, then whisk in the lukewarm gelatine mixture and the baking essence. Continue whisking until the cream is quite thick, then add the sieved icing sugar, vanillin sugar and hazelnuts. Unroll the cooled sponge very carefully and spread evenly with the nut cream filling (leave a little for decorating the outside). Roll up again. Coat the roll with the rest of the cream and sprinkle with hazelnut slices.

SMALL CAKES

Sponge fingers

Sponge mixture:
2 egg yolks
2 well heaped tbsp. sugar
1 packet Oetker Vanillin Sugar
2 egg whites
5 level tbsp. plain flour
3 slightly heaped tbsp. Oetker Gustin (corn starch powder)
1 level tsp. (3 g) Oetker Baking Powder Backin

Whisk the egg yolks a little, then add gradually $2/3$ of the sugar and the vanillin sugar: continue whisking until the mixture is thick and creamy. Whisk the egg whites in a separate bowl until stiff enough to show and retain the cut of a knife, then gradually whisk in the rest of the sugar. Fill the egg white snow onto the egg yolk mixture; mix together the flour, Gustin and Backin and sieve onto the egg whites; fold all gently together (do not stir or beat). Grease a baking sheet and dust lightly with flour; pipe the mixture onto it in finger shapes (not too large as the sponge mixture will rise) and bake immediately.

Oven: pre-heat for 5 minutes at very hot, bake at moderately hot.
Baking time: about 10 minutes.

Moors' Heads

Sponge mixture:
3 egg yolks
1 tbsp. warm water
5½ oz. (150 g) sugar
1 packet Oetker Vanillin Sugar
3 egg whites
5½ oz. (150 g) plain flour
5 slightly heaped tbsp. Oetker Gustin
    (corn starch powder)
1 level tsp. (3 g) Oetker Baking
    Powder Backin

Filling:
1 packet Oetker Pudding Powder,
    vanilla flavour
2 well heaped tbsp. sugar
¾ pt. (425 ccm) and 5 tbsp. cold milk

For brushing:
2 tbsp. apricot jam
    (rubbed through a sieve)

Icing:
7 oz. (200 g) icing sugar
3 level tbsp. cocoa
3–4 tbsp. hot water
¾ oz. (20 g) butter or coconut butter
    (melted)

For the sponge mixture, whisk the egg yolks and the water until frothy, then add gradually ²/₃ of the sugar and the vanillin sugar; continue whisking until the mixture is thick and creamy. Whisk the egg whites in a separate bowl until stiff enough to show and retain the cut of a knife, then gradually whisk in the rest of the sugar. Fill the egg white snow onto the egg yolk mixture; mix together the flour, Gustin and Backin and sieve over the egg whites; fold all gently together (do not beat or stir). Grease a baking sheet and dust lightly with flour; use two teaspoons or a forcing bag to place little heaps (diameter 1–2 in.; 3–5 cm) evenly, but not too closely, on a baking sheet. Bake immediately.
Oven: pre-heat for 5 minutes at very hot,
    bake at moderately hot.
Baking time: 10–15 minutes.
For the filling, blend the pudding powder and the sugar with the 5 tbsp. of milk. Bring the rest of the milk to the boil; remove from heat and gradually stir in the prepared pudding powder; return to heat and boil up briefly. Set aside to cool, stirring now and again. Coat the underside of each of one half of the biscuits thickly with the pudding and place another biscuit on top.
Warm the jam and brush over the cakes.
For the icing, sieve together the cocoa and icing sugar and blend with as much water as will give a good coating consistency, add the hot fat and ice the cakes with the chocolate icing.

CHOUX PASTRY

IMPORTANT PREPARATIONS

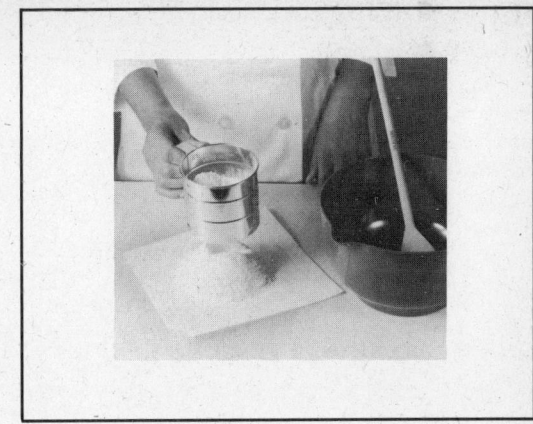

1. **Sieve together the flour and the Gustin.**
   Sieving loosens and aerates the flour and Gustin.

2. **Choux pastry should be baked on a greased baking sheet which has been lightly dusted with flour.**
   a) Sieve a little flour along one side of the baking sheet.

   b) Tip the sheet and tap lightly with the lower edge on the table so that the flour falls and sticks thinly and evenly to the greased sheet. Remove the surplus flour.

CAKE MIXING METHOD

Bring the water and fat to the boil, if possible in a pan with a longish handle. Remove from heat and add the prepared flour and Gustin all at once; stir until a smooth lump forms. Return to heat and heat for 1 minute stirring all the time. Transfer the lump at once to a bowl and beat in the eggs, one at a time. When the mixture is very glossy and hangs from the spoon in long points no more eggs need be added. Add the Backin to the choux mixture which now should be cool.

EIGHT SIMPLE STEPS

1. "Bring the water and fat to the boil, if possible in a pan with a longish handle. Remove from heat and add the prepared flour and Gustin, all at once..."

It is important that no lumps should be formed when the flour-Gustin mixture is added. Therefore remove the boiling ingredients from heat before adding the flour and Gustin and add the whole amount all at once, never sprinkle in a little at a time.

2. "... stir until a smooth lump forms..."

As soon as the dry ingredients are added to the hot liquid, stir vigorously until a smooth lump has formed.

3. **"Heat the lump for one minute stirring all the time..."**
This heating of the lump makes the pastry firmer. When a thin skin forms on the bottom of the pan it has been heated long enough. Use a strong heat for this.

4. **"Transfer the hot mass to a bowl at once..."**
The hot lump is transferred to a bowl so that it will cool more quickly.

5. **"... and beat in the eggs, one at a time..."**
The eggs are added to the hot mixture. Break each egg into a cup first to ensure that it is fresh. The eggs should be added one at a time so that they are more easily absorbed into the mixture.

6. **"When the mixture is very glossy and hangs from the spoon in long points no more eggs need be added..."**
No rule can be given about the exact number of eggs because they vary in size, therefore test the mixture after each egg has been beaten in; if it is very glossy and hangs from the spoon in long points no more eggs should be added, because if the choux mixture becomes too soft the cake will run out of shape. It may be necessary to whisk the last egg and add part of it in order to obtain the proper consistency.

7. **"Add the Backin to the choux mixture which should by now be cool."**
Backin must never be added to warm ingredients as then its rising powder would be activated too early and would thus be lost. This is the reason why the Backin is not mixed with the flour as for other cake mixtures, but is added last of all.

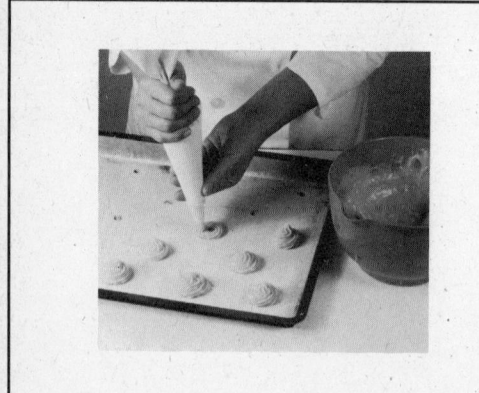

8. For Cream Puffs use two teaspoons to place little heaps of choux mixture on the prepared baking sheet; or the mixture can be filled into a forcing bag and piped onto the sheet. If the pastry is to be cooked in deep fat, the portions should be formed with two teaspoons or piped onto small pieces of greaseproof paper in the form of rings; then they should be removed into the hot fat (e.g. Eberswalder pastries).

BAKING CHOUX PASTRY

Bake each cake according to the instructions in the recipes. Do not open the oven until the cakes are almost finished, and then only carefully, otherwise they may collapse. If the cakes are to be cooked in deep fat, heat the fat well first so that they will not soak in too much fat. Test wether the fat is of the correct temperature by holding a wooden spoon handle down in the fat. If little bubbles form around it the temperature is correct.

CAKES ON A BAKING SHEET

Eclairs

Choux pastry:
1/2 pt. (285 ccm) water
1 3/4 oz. (50 g) butter, margarine or lard
5 1/2 oz. (150 g) plain flour
4 slightly heaped tbsp. Oetker Gustin (corn starch powder)
4–6 eggs
1 level tsp. (3 g) Oetker Baking Powder Backin

Coffee cream filling:
1 1/2 level tsp. Oetker Regina Gelatine, ground white
1 tbsp. cold water for blending
1/2 packet Oetker Pudding Powder, chocolate flavour
2 level – 2 well heaped tbsp. sugar
2/3 pt. (375 ccm) cold milk
1 well heaped tsp. instant coffee powder

Icing:
3 1/2 oz. (100 g) icing sugar
2 level tbsp. cocoa
1–2 tbsp. hot water

For the choux pastry, mix and sieve together the flour and the Gustin. Bring the water and fat to the boil, preferably in a pan with a longish handle. Remove from heat and add the flour and Gustin all at once; stir until a smooth lump forms, heat again for one minute, stirring all the time. Transfer the lump at once into a bowl and beat in the eggs one at a time; when the mixture is very glossy and hangs from the spoon in long points, no more eggs need be added.

Grease a baking sheet and dust lightly with flour. Fill the choux pastry into a forcing bag with a wide nozzle and pipe two finger long strips close to each other then another in the middle on top.

Oven: pre-heat for 5 minutes at very hot,
bake at moderately hot.

Baking time: about 20 minutes.

Cut the eclairs through as soon as they have been baked.

For the coffee cream filling, blend the gelatine with the water and leave ten minutes to swell. Blend the pudding powder and the sugar with 4 tbsp. of the milk and bring the rest of the milk to the boil; remove from heat; stir in slowly the blended pudding powder; return to heat and boil up briefly. Add the swelled gelatine and the instant coffee powder and stir until everything is dissolved. Stir now and again while the cream cools. Fill the eclairs with the cold filling.

For the icing, sieve together the cocoa and the icing sugar and blend with as much of the water as will give a good coating consistency. Ice the eclairs with the chocolate icing.

Cream Puffs (Phot. page 72)

Choux pastry:
1/2 pt. (285 ccm) water
1 3/4 oz. (50 g) butter, margarine or lard
5 1/2 oz. (150 g) plain flour
4 slightly heaped tbsp. Oetker Gustin (corn starch powder)
4–6 eggs
1 level tsp. (3 g) Oetker Baking Powder Backin

Filling (1):
2 level tsp. Oetker Regina Gelatine, ground white
2 tbsp. cold water for blending
4 slightly heaped tbsp. Oetker Gustin (corn starch powder)
2 well heaped tbsp. sugar
3/4 pt. (425 ccm) and 5 tbsp. cold milk
1/2 pt. (285 ccm) fresh double cream
2 packets Oetker Vanillin Sugar

or

Filling (2):
1 1/8 lb. (500 g) morello cherries
2–3 slightly heaped tbsp. sugar
2 slightly heaped tbsp. Oetker Gustin (corn starch powder)
2 level tsp. Oetker Regina Gelatine, ground white
3 tbsp. cold water for blending
1 pt. (570 g) fresh double cream
1 well heaped tbsp. icing sugar
1 packet Oetker Vanillin Sugar

For dusting:
a little icing sugar

For the choux pastry, mix and sieve together the flour and the Gustin. Bring water and fat to the boil, if possible in a pan with a longish handle. Remove from heat and add the flour and Gustin all at once; stir until a smooth lump forms; heat again for one minute stirring all the time. Transfer the lump at once to a bowl and beat in the eggs one at a time. When the mixture is very glossy and hangs from the spoon in long points, no more eggs need be added. Add the Backin to the choux mixture which should now be cool.
Grease a baking sheet and dust lightly with flour. Using two teaspoons or a forcing bag, place small heaps, the size of a walnut on the baking sheet.

Oven: pre-heat for 5 minutes at very hot, bake at moderately hot.

Baking time: 25–30 minutes.
Do not open the oven door during the first quarter of an hour's baking time otherwise the cakes may collapse. As soon as the puffs are baked, cut them open.

For the filling (1), blend the gelatine with the water and leave ten minutes to swell. Blend the Gustin and the sugar with the 5 tbsp. of milk; bring the rest of the milk to the boil; remove from heat; stir in the blended Gustin mixture slowly then boil up again briefly. Stir in the soaked gelatine and continue stirring until it is quite dissolved. Set aside to cool, stirring now and again. Whip the cream until thick, sweeten with the vanillin sugar, then fold into the cold Gustin blancmange.
Fill the puffs with this cream and place the tops back on again.

For the filling (2), wash and stone the cherries, mix them with a well heaped tbsp. sugar and set aside for a while until juice has formed. Bring them then just to boiling point and drain in a sieve or colander catching the juice below. When cherries and juice are cold, measure off 1/4 pt. (if necessary make up the amount with water). Blend with the Gustin; bring to the boil, stirring all the time and boil up briefly. Stir in the cherries; cool well through, then sweeten to taste. Blend the gelatine with the water and leave 10 minutes to swell; warm carefully, stirring all the time, until the gelatine is dissolved, then cool. Whip the cream until almost

Continuation s. page 147

thick, whisk in the lukewarm gelatine solution, the sieved icing sugar and the vanillin sugar and continue whisking until the cream is thick.

Fill each puff, first with a finger-thick layer of cooled cherries, then a layer of cream, then replace the top. Dust the puffs with icing sugar.

Cheese Puffs

Choux pastry:
1/4 pt. (140 ccm) water
1 oz. (30 g) butter or margarine
a pinch of salt
3 slightly heaped tbsp. Oetker Gustin (corn starch powder)
2 1/2 oz. (75 g) plain flour
2–3 eggs
1/2 level tsp. (3 g) Oetker Baking Powder Backin

Cheese cream filling:
4 1/2 oz. (125 g) butter
3 1/2 oz. (100 g) Roquefort or Danish Blue
1 slightly heaped tsp. Oetker Regina Gelatine, ground white
1 tbsp. cold water
1/4 pt. (140 ccm) fresh double cream

For sprinkling:
chopped parsley
caraway seeds
poppy seeds

For the choux pastry, mix and sieve together the flour and the Gustin. Bring the water, fat and salt to the boil, preferably in a pan with a longish handle. Remove from heat and add the flour and Gustin all at once; stir until a smooth lump forms; heat again for one minute, stirring all the time. Transfer the lump at once into a bowl and beat in the eggs one at a time. When the mixture is very glossy and hangs from the spoon in long points no more eggs need be added. Add the Backin to the choux mixture, which should now be cool.

Grease a baking sheet and dust lightly with flour. Fill the choux mixture onto a forcing bag with a small star nozzle and pipe little shapes the size of half a walnut, onto the baking sheet.

Oven: pre-heat for 5 minutes at very hot,
bake at moderately hot.

Baking time: about 20 minutes.

As soon as they are baked cut a small top off each puff.

For the cheese cream filling, cream the butter. Crush the cheese in a bowl and cream it too; beat into the butter a little at a time. Blend the gelatine with the water and leave 10 minutes to swell; warm carefully, stirring all the time, until the gelatine is completely dissolved, then cool. Mix the lukewarm gelatine solution with the cream and whip it until thick; fold this into the butter-cheese mixture. Fill the puffs with the cheese cream, replace the top, coat the puff thinly with cream and sprinkle with parsley, caraway seeds and poppy seeds.

BAKING OR FRYING IN DEEP FAT

Two factors are most important in contributing to the success of this type of cake. They are:
1. careful selection of fat
2. correct temperature of fat when baking

Use oil on its own, never mix it with a hard fat. On the other hand practice has shown that hard fats are best mixed, vegetable and animal fats combined. Suitable combinations are a third coconut butter, a third lard and a third beef dripping.

Heat the fat if possible in an iron or stainless steel pan and make sure there is sufficient fat in it for the cakes to be able to float. When frying the cake mixture, the fat should be neither too hot nor too cold. If it is too hot the cake will brown too quickly, not rise sufficiently and will be raw inside. If the fat is too cool, the cake will absorb too much fat; also the fat may begin to foam as soon as the cake is laid in it. If fat should begin to foam, increase the heat, and take care when dropping in more cakes as this inevitably cools the fat. It is safest to test the fat temperature before placing a new batch of cakes in it. To do this, place the handle of a wooden spoon in the fat; if bubbles form round it the fat is hot enough.

Eberswalder Pastries (Phot. page 35)

Choux pastry:
1/2 pt. (285 ccm) water
1 3/4 oz. (50 g) butter or margarine
5 1/2 oz. (150 g) plain flour
4 slightly heaped tbsp. Oetker Gustin (corn starch powder)
1 well heaped tbsp. sugar
1 packet Oetker Vanillin Sugar
4–6 eggs
1 level tsp. (3 g) Oetker Baking Powder Backin

For frying:
oil, lard or coconut butter

Icing:
7 oz. (200 g) icing sugar
4 drops Oetker Baking Essence, lemon flavour
about 4 tbsp. hot water

For the pastry, mix and sieve together the flour and the Gustin. Bring water and fat to the boil, preferably in a pan with a longish handle. Remove from heat and add the flour and Gustin all at once; stir until a smooth lump forms, then heat again for a minute, stirring all the time. Transfer the lump to a bowl and gradually beat in the sugar, the vanillin sugar and the eggs one at a time. When the mixture is very glossy and hangs from the spoon in long points, no more eggs need be added. Add the Backin to the choux mixture which should now be cool.

Fill the mixture into a forcing bag with a wide nozzle and pipe it in rings onto squares of greaseproof paper (4 1/2 in. – 10,10 cm) which have been greased with butter or margarine. When the paper is dipped into the hot fat, the cake slides off. Fry them on both sides until golden brown. Remove the cakes with a skimming ladle and drain them well.

For the icing, sieve the icing sugar and blend with the lemon flavour and as much water as will give a good coating consistency. Ice the pastries with this.

Berlin Pancakes (Phot. page 35)

Ingredients:
Cottage cheese pastry (2) see page 70
For brushing:
a little milk
Filling:
about 5½ oz. (150 g) jam
For frying:
oil, lard or coconut butter
For dusting:
a little icing sugar

Roll out the pastry about ¼ in. (½ cm) thick. Using a round pastry cutter (diameter: 3¼–4 in. – 8–9 cm)·mark circles on one half of the pastry without actually cutting out. Brush over the edges of the circles thinly with milk and place a little jam in the middle. Tip over the empty half of the pastry and cut out the rounds, pressing the edges well together. Fry them right away in hot fat on both sides until golden brown. Remove with a skimming ladle, drain by standing on a cake wire, then dust with icing sugar.

Ballbäuschen

Ingredients:
3½ oz. (100 g) butter or margarine
2 well heaped tbsp. sugar
1 packet Oetker Vanillin Sugar
2 eggs
9 oz. (250 g) plain flour
2 level tsp. (6 g) Oetker Baking Powder Backin
about 4 tbsp. milk
For frying:
oil, lard or coconut butter
For dusting:
a little icing sugar

Cream the fat and gradually add the sugar, the vanillin sugar and the eggs. Mix and sieve together the flour and the Backin and add to the creamed ingredients alternately with the milk. Use only so much milk as will give a mixture of a heavy dropping consistency. Using a teaspoon previously dipped in the hot fat, spoon small balls of the cake mixture into the hot fat. Fry on both sides in hot fat until golden brown. Remove with a skimming ladle, drain well and dust with icing sugar.

Twists

Ingredients:
1⅛ lb. (500 g) plain flour
1 level tsp. (3 g) Oetker Baking Powder Backin
3½ oz. (100 g) sugar
a few drops Oetker Baking Essence, lemon flavour
1 bottle Oetker rum flavour
3 eggs
4 tbsp. milk or water
4½ oz. (125 g) butter or margarine
For frying:
oil, lard or coconut butter
For dusting:
a little icing sugar

Mix together the flour and the Backin and sieve onto a pastry board or cool slab. Make a well in the centre and pour in the sugar, the flavourings, the eggs and the liquid. Draw in some of the flour from the sides of the well to mix with these to form a thickish paste. Add the cold fat, cut into small pieces. Cover the whole with more of the flour and starting from the middle, work all these ingredients quickly with the hands into a firm smooth paste. Roll out thinly and cut into strips with a pastry cutter. Make a slit in the middle and draw one end through.

Fry the twists in hot fat until golden brown; remove with a skimming ladle and drain well, then dust with icing sugar.

Mutzenmandeln (Phot. page 35)

Ingredients:
1¹/₈ lb. (500 g) plain flour
2 level tsp. (6 g) Oetker Baking Powder Backin
5¹/₂ oz. (150 g) sugar
3–4 drops Oetker Baking Essence, bitter almond flavour
1 bottle Oetker rum flavour
3 eggs
5¹/₂ oz. (150 g) butter or margarine
For frying:
oil, lard or coconut butter
For tossing:
a little castor sugar

Mix together the flour and the Backin and sieve onto a pastry board or cool slab. Make a well in the centre and pour in the sugar, flavourings and eggs. Draw in some of the flour from the sides of the well to mix with these to form a thickish paste. Add the cold fat, cut into small pieces. Cover the whole with more of the flour and, starting from the middle, work all these ingredients quickly with the hands into a smooth firm paste. If it should stick cool well through for some time. Roll out the pastry about ¹/₂ in. (1 cm) thick and cut out Mutzenmandel shapes and fry these in hot fat until golden. Remove with a skimming ladle, drain well and toss in castor sugar while still hot.

TRADITIONAL GERMAN CHRISTMAS RECIPES (Phot. page 92)

HONEY CAKES

Some of the best German Christmas recipes are those in which the ingredients honey or treacle play an important part. This is partly because of the delicious taste they impart, but also because biscuits and cakes containing honey or treacle may be stored for some considerable time.
Honey or treacle should, as a general rule, be melted slowly together with the sugar and fat. It may be of advantage to add some or all of the liquid mentioned in a recipe so that the sugar will melt more quickly. These ingredients should not be warmed over too strong a heat; either melt them in a double saucepan, or keep the heat low and stir all the time. As soon as everything is melted, remove from the heat and place the saucepan or bowl, depending on the recipe, in cold water. Stir frequently during this cooling process so that the honey or treacle mass cools evenly. It is important that the melted ingredients should be cooled to blood heat, because otherwise the Backin would be activated too early and the rising, which should take place during baking, would begin during the mixing.

Domino Cubes

Ingredients:
9 oz. (250 g) honey
2¼ oz. (65 g) sugar
2¼ oz. (65 g) butter or margarine
2 eggs
4 drops Oetker Baking Essence, lemon flavour
a good pinch ground cardamom
a good pinch ground cloves
1 level tsp. ground cinnamon
10½ oz. (300 g) plain flour
2 level tbsp. cocoa
3 level tsp. (9 g) Oetker Baking Powder Backin

Filling:
about 1 lb. (450 g) redcurrant jelly

Icing:
1⅛ lb. (500 g) icing sugar
5 level tbsp. cocoa
about 8 tbsp. hot milk
1¾ oz. (50 g) coconut butter (melted)

For the cake mixture, warm the honey, sugar and fat slowly, melting them carefully. Transfer to a mixing bowl and cool; when almost cold mix in the eggs, flavouring and spices. Mix and sieve together the flour, cocoa and the Backin and add these gradually to the melted ingredients. Grease a baking sheet and spread the cake mixture about 1¼ in. (1½ cm) thick over it (if the baking sheet is 12×18 in. (32×46 cm) ⅔ of its surface will be covered). Place a folded piece of greaseproof paper in front of the cake mixture at the open end of the sheet.
Oven: moderately hot.
Baking time: 20–25 minutes.
When the cake is cold cut into 1 in. (2½ cm) squares; halve these horizontally and spread with the redcurrant jelly. Replace the tops and turn them so that the smoothest side is at the top; coat the sides and top thinly with jelly.
For the icing, sieve together the icing sugar and the cocoa and blend with as much milk as will give a good coating consistency. Add the hot fat.
Ice the domino cubes with the chocolate icing; place the icing in the meantime over hot water so that it will remain liquid.

Honey-Bread

Ingredients:
9 oz. (250 g) honey
7 oz. (200 g) sugar
2¼ oz. (65 g) butter or margarine
almost ¼ pt. (140 ccm) malt beer
1 egg
½ level tsp. ground cardamom
½ level tsp. ground cloves
1 level tsp. ground cinnamon
1 bottle Oetker rum flavour
6 drops Oetker Baking Essence, lemon flavour
3 drops Oetker Baking Essence, bitter almond flavour
1⅛ lb. (500 g) plain flour
1 packet Oetker Baking Powder Backin

Icing:
3½ oz. (100 g) icing sugar
about 2 tbsp. hot water

For the cake mixture, warm the honey, sugar, fat and beer slowly, melting carefully. Transfer to a mixing bowl and cool. When almost cold, mix in the egg, the flavourings and spices. Mix and sieve together the flour and the Backin and add this gradually to the melted ingredients. Grease a baking sheet and using a plastic spatula spread the cake mixture evenly over the sheet ½ in. (1 cm) thick. Place a folded piece of greaseproof paper against the cake mixture along the open end of the baking sheet.
Oven: moderately hot.
Baking time: about 20 minutes.
For the icing, sieve the icing sugar and blend with as much of the water as will give a good coating consistency. Ice the cake as soon as it is baked and cut into pieces 2×2½ in. (5×6 cm).
Store the honey bread in an airtight tin so that it stays fresh.

Honey Biscuits

Ingredients:
4½ oz. (125 g) honey
7 oz. (200 g) sugar
4 tbsp. milk
3½ oz. (100 g) butter or margarine
1 packet Oetker Vanillin Sugar
3 drops Oetker Baking Essence,
　　bitter almond flavour
1 level tsp. ground cinnamon
14 oz. (400 g) plain flour
2 level tbsp. cocoa
3½ oz. (100 g) Oetker Gustin
　　(corn starch powder)
1 packet Oetker Baking Powder
　　Backin
2½ oz. (75 g) almonds
　　(blanched and chopped)
For brushing:
1 slightly heaped tbsp. potato flour
6 tbsp. water
For decorating:
4½ oz. (125 g) almonds
　　(blanched and split)

For the biscuit mixture, warm the honey, sugar, milk and fat slowly, melting carefully. Transfer to a mixing bowl and cool. Mix and sieve together the flour, cocoa, Gustin and Backin. When the melted ingredients are almost cold, stir in the flavourings and the spices gradually, then ⅔ of the flour. Knead in the rest of the flour and the almonds lightly with the hands. If the paste is sticky, add a little flour.

Roll out the pastry about ¼ in. (½ cm) thick and cut out shapes with a round pastry cutter, diameter 3¼ in. (8 cm). Lay these on a greased baking sheet.

Oven: pre-heat for 5 minutes at very hot,
　　　　bake at moderately hot.
Baking time: about 20 minutes.
For brushing, blend the potato flour with the water, bring to the boil, then cool. Brush over the biscuits thinly and decorate with the split almonds.

Lebkuchen

Ingredients:
1¾ oz. (50 g) butter or margarine
6 oz. (170 g) sugar
1 packet Oetker Vanillin Sugar
1 egg
1 egg yolk
3½ oz. (100 g) honey
½ tsp. ground anniseed
1 level tsp. ground cloves
1 level tsp. ground cinnamon
1⅛ lb. (500 g) plain flour
1 packet Oetker Baking Powder Backin
3 tbsp. milk
Icing:
7 oz. (200 g) icing sugar
1 egg white
about 2 tbsp. lemon juice

For the cake mixture, cream the fat and gradually add the sugar, vanillin sugar, egg, egg yolk, the honey and the spices. Mix and sieve together the flour and the Backin and mix ⅔ of this into the creamed ingredients a little at a time. Knead in the rest of the flour lightly with the hands to form a smooth firm paste. If it should stick, cool well through for some time.

Roll out the pastry about ¼ in. (½ cm) thick and cut out different shapes; lay these on a greased baking sheet.
Oven: pre-heat for 5 minutes at very hot,
　　　　bake at moderately hot.
Baking time: about 10 minutes.
For the icing, sieve the icing sugar and blend with the egg white and as much of the lemon juice as will give a good coating consistency. Ice the cooled biscuits with this.

Filled Honey Cake

Ingredients:
7 oz. (200 g) honey or treacle
3½ oz. (100 g) sugar
a pinch of salt
1¾ oz. (50 g) butter, margarine
 or lard
1 tbsp. water
1 egg
1 level tsp. ground cinnamon
2 drops Oetker Baking Essence,
 bitter almond flavour
1⅛ lb. (500 g) plain flour
1 packet Oetker Baking Powder Backin
Filling:
about 13 oz. (375 g) jam
 (not too sweet)
Icing:
3½ oz. (100 g) icing sugar
1–2 tbsp. lemon juice or water

For the cake mixture, warm the honey or treacle, sugar, salt, fat and water slowly, melting them carefully. Transfer to a mixing bowl and cool. Mix and sieve together the flour and the Backin. When the melted ingredients are almost cold, gradually add the egg, flavouring, spice and ⅓ of the flour. Knead in the rest of the flour lightly with the hands, if it should stick, add a little more flour. Roll out ⅔ of the pastry to fit ¾ of a greased baking sheet 12×18 in. (32×46 cm) and press up a little at the edges. Roll out the rest of the pastry to form a lid, roll it up with a sheet of paper and lay aside. Spread the pastry on the baking sheet evenly with the jam, leaving a small border free around the edges. Lay the pastry lid on top and prick well with a fork.
Oven: pre-heat for 5 minutes at very hot,
 bake at moderately hot.
Baking time: about 20 minutes.
For the icing, sieve the icing sugar and blend with as much of the lemon juice or water as will give a good coating consistency. Ice the cake as soon as it comes out of the oven and cut into even slices of 1×4 in. (3×9 cm).

Brown Christmas Biscuits

Ingredients:
9 oz. (250 g) honey
4½ oz. (125 g) sugar
a pinch of salt
2¼ oz. (65 g) butter or margarine
2¼ oz. (65 g) lard
1 tbsp. milk
5 drops Oetker Baking Essence,
 lemon flavour
1 level tsp. ground cardamom
1⅛ lb. (500 g) plain flour
3 level tsp. (9 g) Oetker Baking
 Powder Backin
1 oz. (30 g) ground hazelnuts
For brushing:
a little tinned milk

Warm the honey, sugar, salt, fat and milk slowly, melting them carefully. Transfer to a mixing bowl and cool; when almost cold mix in the flavouring and the spices. Mix and sieve together the flour and the Backin and add ⅔ of it to the melted ingredients. Knead in the rest of the flour and the nuts lightly with the hands so that a soft dough results. If it should stick, add a little more flour. Roll out the pastry thinly and cut out round, square or rectangular shapes with a pastry cutter. Grease a baking sheet and lay the biscuits on it. Brush them thinly with milk.
Oven: pre-heat for 5 minutes at very hot,
 bake at moderately hot.
Baking time: about 10 minutes.

Liegnitzer Cookies

Ingredients:
14 oz. (400 g) honey
9 oz. (250 g) sugar
4½ oz. (125 g) butter, margarine
   or lard
6 tbsp. milk or water
3 eggs
½ bottle Oetker Baking Essence,
   lemon flavour
a pinch ground cardamom
1 slightly heaped tsp. ground cloves
2 slightly heaped tsp. ground
   cinnamon
1⅛ lb. (500 g) plain flour
5 level tbsp. cocoa
1 packet Oetker Baking Powder Backin
4½ oz. (125 g) currants
   (washed and well drained)
4½ oz. (125 g) almonds (chopped)
5½ oz. (150 g) candied lemon peel
   (diced)

For brushing:
7–9 oz. (200–250 g) apricot jam
about 2 tbsp. water

Icing:
12 oz. (350 g) icing sugar
3 level tbsp. cocoa
about 4 tbsp. hot water

For the cookie mixture, warm the honey, sugar, fat and liquid slowly melting them carefully. Transfer to a mixing bowl and cool. Mix and sieve together the flour, cocoa and Backin. When the melted ingredients are almost cold, mix in the eggs, flavouring and spices, flour, currants almonds and candied peel. Grease a baking sheet and place greased metal rings, diameter 2 in. (6 cm), height 1–1½ in. (3–4 cm) on it. Fill these half full of cake mixture.

Oven: moderately hot.
Baking time: 20–25 minutes.

Mix the jam with the water and boil up. Brush thinly over the cooled cookies.

For the icing, sieve together the icing sugar and the cocoa and blend with as much water as will give a good coating consistency. Ice the cookies.

Paving Stones

Ingredients:
9 oz. (250 g) honey or treacle
3½ oz. (100 g) sugar
a pinch of salt
1 tbsp. oil
2 tbsp. water
2 egg yolks
½ egg white
4 drops Oetker Baking Essence,
   bitter almond flavour
3 drops Oetker Baking Essence,
   lemon flavour

For the biscuit mixture, warm the honey or treacle, sugar, salt, oil and water slowly, melting them carefully. Transfer to a mixing bowl and cool. Mix and sieve together the flour and the Backin. When the melted ingredients are almost cold, add the egg yolks gradually, ½ egg white, the flavourings and spices and ⅔ of the flour. Knead in the rest of the flour, the nuts and the candied peel lightly by hand so that a smooth firm paste results. Form the pastry into rolls as thick as a thumb and from these cut off small pieces, form these into balls the size of cherries. Grease a baking sheet and place 8–12 of these balls not too close together inside a greased

Continued on next page

1 heaped tsp. cocoa
1 level tsp. ground cloves
1 level tsp. ground cinnamon
1¹/₈ lb. (500 g) plain flour
1 packet Oetker Baking Powder Backin
1³/₄ oz. (50 g) almonds (blanched
    and finely chopped)
  or hazelnuts (finely chopped)
³/₄ oz. (20 g) candied orange or
    lemon peel (finely diced)
Icing:
1¹/₂ egg whites
7–8 oz. (200–225 g) icing sugar

metal ring, diameter 3¹/₄ in. (8 cm). These rings may be made from a strip of greaseproof paper about 12 in. (30 cm) long which can be held together in a ring shape with a paper clip or with thread.
Oven: moderately hot.
Baking time: 20–25 minutes.
Do not bake the biscuits too long!
For the icing, blend the egg whites with as much of the sieved icing sugar as will give a good coating consistency. Ice the biscuits with this while they are still hot.

Honey Buttons

Ingredients:
9 oz. (250 g) honey or treacle
3¹/₂ oz. (100 g) sugar
1³/₄ oz. (50 g) butter, margarine
    or lard
1 tbsp. water
1 egg
1 level tsp. ground cinnamon
2 drops Oetker Baking Essence,
    bitter almond flavour
3 drops Oetker Baking Essence,
    lemon flavour
1¹/₈ lb. (500 g) plain flour
4 level tsp. (12 g) Oetker Baking
    Powder Backin
1³/₄ oz. (50 g) almonds
    (blanched and chopped)
  or 1³/₄ oz. (50 g) currants
    (washed and well drained)
1 oz. (30 g) candied orange or lemon
    peel (finely diced)
For brushing:
a little milk
For sprinkling:
coarse – grained sugar

For the biscuit mixture, warm the honey or treacle, sugar, fat and water slowly, melting them carefully. Transfer to a mixing bowl and cool. Mix and sieve together the flour and the Backin. When the melted ingredients are almost cold, add gradually the egg, flavourings, spices and ²/₃ of the flour. Knead in the rest of the flour, the almonds (or currants) and the candied peel lightly with the hands, to form a smooth firm paste. If it should stick, add a little flour. Form the pastry into rolls as thick as a thumb and cut off small pieces, form these into cherry sized balls. Flatten these slightly, brush with milk, press the damp surface into the sugar and place on a greased baking sheet.
Oven: pre-heat for 5 minutes at very hot,
         bake at moderately hot.
Baking time: 10–20 minutes.
After baking the honey buttons leave them in the air for a few days so that they become softer.

Nussprinten

Ingredients:
4½ oz. (125 g) treacle
2 well heaped tbsp. sugar
1¾ oz. (50 g) butter or margarine
2 tbsp. milk or water
1¾ oz. (50 g) brown sugar candy
   (pounded into small pieces)
3 drops Oetker Baking Essence,
   lemon flavour
½ level tsp. ground anniseed
½ level tsp. ground cloves
½ level tsp. ground cinnamon
9 oz. (250 g) plain flour
3 level tsp. (9 g) Oetker Baking
   Powder Backin

For decorating:
about 7 oz. (200 g) hazelnuts (halved)

Icing:
7 oz. (200 g) icing sugar
3 level tbsp. cocoa
2–3 tbsp. hot water

For the biscuit mixture, warm the treacle, sugar, fat and liquid slowly, melting carefully. Transfer to a mixing bowl and cool. Mix and sieve together the flour and Backin. When the melted ingredients are almost cold, mix in the sugar candy, the flavouring, spices and ⅔ of the flour. Knead in the rest of the flour to form a smooth paste. If it should stick, cool well through for an hour.

Roll out the pastry about ¼ in. (½ cm) thick and cut out rectangles of 1 × 3 in. (2½ × 7 cm). Place on a greased baking sheet and cover the top surface with halved hazelnuts.

Oven: pre-heat for 5 minutes at very hot,
           bake at moderately hot.

Baking time: about 10 minutes.

For the icing, sieve together the icing sugar and cocoa and blend with as much of the water as will give a good coating consistency. Ice the cooled Nußprinten.

Spitz Cakes

Ingredients:
6 oz. (170 g) honey or treacle
2 well heaped tbsp. sugar
pinch of salt
2 tbsp. oil
1 egg
1 heaped tsp. cocoa
6 drops Oetker Baking Essence,
   lemon flavour
a good pinch ground allspice
1 level tsp. ground cinnamon
9 oz. (250 g) plain flour
3 level tsp. (9 g) Oetker Baking
   Powder Backin
2½ oz. (70 g) almonds (blanched
   and finely chopped)

For brushing:
4½ oz. (125 g) redcurrant jelly

For the cake mixture, warm the honey, sugar, salt and oil slowly, melting carefully. Transfer to a mixing bowl and cool. Mix and sieve together the flour and the Backin. Gradually add the egg, cocoa, flavouring and spices and ⅔ of the flour to the cooled melted ingredients. Knead in the rest of the flour and the almonds lightly with the hands so that a smooth firm paste results. If it should stick cool well through for some time.

Form rolls from the pastry ¾ in. (2 cm) thick and as long as the baking sheet. Lay them, not too close together, on the greased sheet, flatten slightly and bake golden brown.

Oven: pre-heat for 5 minutes at very hot,
           bake at moderately hot.

Baking time: about 20 minutes.

After baking cut the cooled rolls into triangles. Coat these with the heated jelly and brush over with the chocolate icing.

Continued on next page

Icing:
9 oz. (250 g) icing sugar
3 level tbsp. cocoa
3–4 tbsp. hot milk
1 oz. (30 g) coconut butter (melted)

For the icing, sieve together the icing sugar and the cocoa and blend with as much of the milk as will give a good coating consistency. Add the hot fat.

Nürnberger Lebkuchen

Ingredients:
6 oz. (170 g) honey or treacle
2 well heaped tbsp. sugar
a pinch of salt
2 tbsp. oil
2 tbsp. water
1 egg yolk
1 heaped tsp. cocoa
6 drops Oetker Baking Essence, lemon flavour
a good pinch ground allspice
1 level tsp. ground cinnamon
9 oz. (250 g) plain flour
3 level tsp. (9 g) Oetker Baking Powder Backin
2½ oz. (70 g) almonds (ground)
2½ oz. (70 g) hazelnuts (ground)
1¾ oz. (50 g) candied lemon peel (diced)
2½ oz. (70 g) dried apricots (cut into small pieces)
Icing:
4½ oz. (125 g) icing sugar
1 egg white
possibly a few drops of water
For sprinkling:
if desired, coloured sugar

For the biscuit mixture, warm the honey or treacle, sugar, salt, oil and water slowly, melting them carefully. Transfer to a mixing bowl and cool. Mix and sieve together the flour and the Backin. Mix the egg yolk, cocoa, flavouring and spices and ⅔ of the flour gradually into the cooled melted ingredients. Knead in the rest of the flour, the almonds, hazelnuts, candied peel and apricots lightly with the hands so that a firm smooth paste results. Roll out the pastry ¼ in. (½ cm) thick and cut out round shapes, diameter 3¼ in. (8 cm) or oblongs 4 × 2½ in. (9 × 6 cm). Lay these on a greased baking sheet.
Oven: pre-heat for 5 minutes at very hot,
bake at moderately hot.
Baking time: 15–20 minutes.
For the icing, blend the sieved icing sugar with the egg white. If it is still too thick, add a few drops of water. Ice the biscuits thinly with the icing and sprinkle with the coloured sugar.

PASTRY-TYPE CAKES AND BISCUITS

Spekulatius (Phot. page 128)

Pastry (1):
1¹/₈ lb. (500 g) plain flour
3 level tsp. (9 g) Oetker Baking Powder Backin
7 oz. (200 g) sugar, a pinch of salt
1 packet Oetker Vanillin Sugar
3 drops Oetker Baking Essence, bitter almond flavour
1 bottle Oetker rum flavour
1 level tsp. cocoa
2 good pinches ground cloves
1 level tsp. ground cinnamon
1 egg, 2 tbsp. milk
4¹/₂ oz. (125) butter, margarine or lard

or

Pastry (2):
1¹/₈ lb. (500 g) plain flour
2 level tsp. (6 g) Oetker Baking Powder Backin
9 oz. (250 g) sugar
1 packet Oetker Vanillin Sugar
2 drops Oetker Baking Essence, bitter almond flavour
2 good pinches ground cardamom
2 good pinches ground cloves
1 level tsp. ground cinnamon
2 eggs
7 oz. (200 g) butter or margarine
3¹/₂ oz. (100 g) almonds or hazelnuts (ground)

Mix and sieve together the flour and the Backin onto a pastry board or cool slab. Make a well in the centre and pour in the sugar, flavourings, spices, egg (or eggs) and milk. Draw in some of the flour from the sides of the well to mix with these to form a thickish paste. Add the cold fat, cut into small pieces (and for Pastry (2) the nuts). Cover the whole with more of the flour and, starting from the middle, work all these ingredients quickly with the hands into a firm smooth paste. If it should stick, cool well through for some time.

Roll out the biscuit pastry thinly and cut out different shapes (if possible animal shapes) with a pastry cutter and lay these on a greased baking sheet. If the special Spekulatius wooden mould is used, flour it well, press in the pastry, cut away the surplus pastry and tap the biscuit shape carefully out of the mould.

Oven: pre-heat for 5 minutes at very hot, bake at moderately hot.
Baking time: about 10 minutes.

Iced Spice Nuts

Pastry:
1¹/₈ lb. (500 g) plain flour
3 level tsp. (9 g) Oetker Baking Powder Backin
11¹/₂ oz. (325 g) sugar

For the biscuit mixture, mix and sieve together the flour and the Backin onto a pastry board or cool slab. Make a well in the centre and pour in the sugar, the flavourings and spices, eggs and the liquid. Draw some of the flour from the sides of the well to combine with these to form a thickish paste. Add the almonds and the

Continued on next page

½ bottle Oetker Baking Essence,
    lemon flavour
2 good pinches each of:
    ground ginger
    ground cardamom
    ground cloves
    ground allspice
    ground white pepper
1 slightly heaped tsp. ground cinnamon
2 eggs, 6 tbsp. milk or water
1¾ oz. (50 g) almonds (ground)
1¾ oz. (50 g) candied lemon peel
    (very finely diced)
Icing:
8 oz. (225 g) icing sugar
about 3 tbsp. hot water

candied peel and cover the whole with more of the flour. Starting from the middle work all these ingredients quickly with the hands into a firm smooth paste. If it should stick add a little more flour.
Roll out the pastry ½ in. (1 cm) thick and cut out small round shapes diameter 1 in. (2½ cm) with a pastry cutter. Lay these on a greased baking sheet.
Oven: pre-heat for 5 minutes at very hot,
        bake at moderately hot.
Baking time: about 15 minutes.
For the icing, sieve the icing sugar and blend with as much water as will give a good coating consistency. Coat the cooled spice nuts with this icing. If they are hard, leave them in the air for a few days, then store in an airtight tin.

Vanilla Crescents (uses up leftover egg yolks)

Pastry:
9 oz. (250 g) plain flour
a pinch of Oetker Baking Powder Backin
4½ oz. (125 g) sugar
1 packet Oetker Vanillin Sugar
3 egg yolks
7 oz. (200 g) butter or margarine
4½ oz. (125 g) almonds
    (blanched and ground)
For tossing:
1 slighlty heaped tbsp. icing sugar
1 packet Oetker Vanillin Sugar

Mix and sieve together the flour and the Backin onto a pastry board or cool slab. Make a well in the centre and pour in the sugar, vanillin sugar and egg yolks. Draw in some of the flour from the sides of the well to mix with these to form a thickish paste. Add the cold fat, cut into small pieces and the almonds. Cover the whole with more of the flour and, working from the middle combine all these ingredients quickly with the hands into a firm smooth paste. If it should stick, cool well through for some time. Form the pastry into rolls as thick as a thumb; cut these into 1 in. (2 cm) pieces. Form these into 2 in. (5 cm) rolls with the ends a little thinner than the middle. Lay these in crescent shapes on a baking sheet and bake them till golden.
Oven: pre-heat for 5 minutes at very hot,
        bake at moderately hot.
Baking time: about 10 minutes.
Sieve the icing sugar and mix with the vanillin sugar. Toos the vanilla sugar. Toss the vanilla crescents in this while they are still hot.

Nut Cookies

Pastry:
9 oz. (250 g) plain flour
1 level tsp. Oetker Baking Powder Backin
5½ oz. (150 g) sugar
1 packet Oetker Vanillin Sugar
3 drops Oetker Baking Essence,
   bitter almond flavour
4 tbsp. milk
3½ oz. (100 g) butter or margarine
7 oz. (200 g) hazelnuts (ground twice)
For brushing:
a little milk or tinned milk
For decorating:
1–1½ oz. (30–40 g) hazelnuts
   (halved)

Mix and sieve together the flour and the Backin onto a pastry board or cool slab. Make a well in the centre and pour in the sugar, the vanillin sugar, the flavourings and the milk. Draw in some of the flour from the sides of the well to combine with these to form a thickish paste. Add the cold fat, cut into small pieces and the hazelnuts. Cover the whole with more of the flour and, starting from the middle, work all these ingredients quickly with the hands into a smooth firm paste. If it should stick, cool well through for some time.
Roll out the biscuit pastry, in small quantities, about ⅛ in. (3 mm) thick and cut out round shapes. Lay these on a baking sheet, brush with milk and decorate each with half a hazelnut.
Oven: pre-heat for 5 minutes at very hot,
   bake at moderately hot.
Baking time: 10–15 minutes.

Stollen (German Christmas Cake)

Cake Mixture:
1⅛ lb. (500 g) plain flour
1 packet Oetker Baking Powder Backin
7 oz. (200 g) sugar
1 packet Oetker Vanillin Sugar
a pinch of salt
4 drops Oetker Baking Essence,
   bitter almond flavour
4 drops Oetker Baking Essence,
   lemon flavour
1 bottle Oetker rum flavour
a good pinch ground cardamom
a good pinch ground mace
2 eggs
4½ oz. (125 g) butter or margarine
1¾ oz. (50 g) beef dripping
9 oz. (250 g) cottage cheese
   (well pressed out)
4½ oz. (125 g) currants
   (washed and well drained)

Mix and sieve together the flour and the Backin onto a pastry board or cool slab. Make a well in the centre and pour in the sugar, vanillin sugar, the flavourings and spices, and the eggs. Draw in some of the flour from the sides of the well to mix with these to form a thickish paste. Add the cold butter or margarine, cut into small pieces, the finely chopped beef dripping, the cottage cheese (if preferred rubbed through a fine sieve) the currants and sultanas, the nuts and the candied peel. Cover the fruit with more of the flour and, starting from the middle, work all these ingredients quickly with the hands into a firm smooth paste. If it should stick, add a little more flour.
Form the mixture into a longish oval shape, then fold it over lengthways to give the traditional "Stollen" shape. Line a baking sheet with greased greaseproof paper and lay the Stollen on this.
Oven: pre-heat for 5 minutes at very hot,
   bake at moderately hot.
Baking time: 50–60 minutes.
Continued on next page

4½–9 oz. (125–250 g) sultanas
  (washed and well drained)
4½–9 oz. (125–250 g) almonds or
  hazelnuts (ground or finely
  chopped)
1¾–3½ oz. (50–100 g) candied
  lemon peel (diced)
For brushing:
1¾ oz. (50 g) butter or margarine
  (melted)
For dusting:
2 well heaped tbsp. icing sugar

As soon as the Stollen comes out of the oven, brush over with the fat and dust thickly with the icing sugar.

CAKES AND BISCUITS MADE WITH WHISKED EGGS OR EGG WHITES

Coconut Macaroons (uses up leftover egg whites)

Ingredients:
4 egg whites
7 oz. (200 g) castor sugar
a good pinch ground cinnamon
2 drops Oetker Baking Essence,
  bitter almond flavour
7 oz. (200 g) desiccated coconut

Whisk the egg whites until stiff enough to show and retain the cut of a knife; then whisk in gradually the sugar, cinnamon and flavouring. Gently fold in the desiccated coconut (do not beat or stir). Grease a baking sheet and use two teaspoons to place little heaps on it.
Oven: slow.
Baking time: 20–25 minutes.

Almond Macaroons (uses up leftover egg whites)

Ingredients:
2 egg whites
3½ oz. (100 g) castor sugar
a good pinch ground cinnamon
2 drops Oetker Baking Essence,
  bitter almond flavour
3½ oz. (100 g) almonds
  (blanched and ground)
2½ oz. (75 g) almonds
  (blanched and chopped)

Whisk the egg whites until stiff enough to show and retain the cut of a knife. Whisk in the sugar gradually, then the cinnamon and flavouring. Finally fold in the almonds gently (do not stir or beat). Grease a baking sheet well and use two teaspoons to place small heaps of the macaroon mixture on the sheet.
Oven: slow.
Baking time: 30–35 minutes.

Nutty Biscuits

Ingredients:
4 tbsp. oil or 2½ oz. (75 g) butter
  or margarine
4½ oz. (125 g) coarse rolled oats
2½ oz. (75 g) sugar
1 egg
3–5 drops Oetker Baking Essence,
  bitter almond flavour
5 level tbsp. plain flour
1 level tsp. (3 g) Oetker Baking
  Powder Backin

Brown the rolled oats slightly in the fat stirring all the time; add 1 tbsp. of the sugar and brown a little longer; set aside to cool. Whisk the egg, gradually add the rest of the sugar and the flavouring and then whisk until the mixture is thick and creamy. Mix and sieve together the flour and the Backin and add this and the well-cooled rolled oats a little at a time to the whisked ingredients. Use two teaspoons to place walnut – sized heaps on a greased baking sheet.
Oven: pre-heat for 5 minutes at very hot,
       bake at moderately hot.
Baking time: 12–15 minutes.

Elise Spice Cookies

Ingredients:
quantity sufficient for about 40 rice
paper wafers, diameter 3 in. (6 cm)
2 eggs
7 oz. (200 g) sugar
1 packet Oetker Vanillin Sugar
a good pinch ground cloves
1 level tsp. ground cinnamon
½ bottle Oetker rum flavour
1–2 drops Oetker Baking Essence,
  lemon flavour
2½ oz. (70 g) candied lemon or
  orange peel (very finely diced)
4½ oz. (125 g) almonds (ground)
a good pinch Oetker Baking Powder
  Backin
2½–4½ oz. (75–125 g) hazelnuts
  (ground)
(exact quantity depends on size of eggs)
White icing:
5½ oz. (150 g) icing sugar
1–2 tbsp. hot water
Dark icing:
3½ oz. (100 g) icing sugar
2 level tbsp. cocoa
1–2 tbsp. hot water
if desired, knob coconut butter (melted)

For the cookie mixture, whisk the eggs until frothy, then gradually add the sugar and the vanillin sugar. Continue whisking for about 15 minutes until the mixture is thick and creamy. Mix the Backin among the almonds. Mix in the flavourings and spices, and the almonds. Add as much of the ground hazelnuts as will give a spreading consistency. Place a heaped tsp. of the mixture on each wafer; smooth this with a knife dipped in water and lay on a baking sheet.
Oven: slow.
Baking time: 25–35 minutes.
For the white icing, sieve the icing sugar and blend with as much of the water as will give a good coating consistency.
For the dark icing, sieve together the icing sugar and the cocoa and blend with as much of the water as will give a good coating consistency. Add the hot fat.
Coat the spice cookies with either the white or dark icing while they are still hot.

Spice Cookies

Ingredients:
3 eggs
7 oz. (200 g) sugar
1 packet Oetker Vanillin Sugar
$1/2$ bottle Oetker rum flavour
1 level tsp. ground cardamom
1 level tsp. ground cloves
1 level tsp. ground cinnamon
7 oz. (200 g) plain flour
a pinch of Oetker Baking Powder Backin

Whisk the eggs until frothy then add gradually the sugar, the flavourings and spices. Continue whisking for about 15 minutes until the mixture is thick and creamy. Mix and sieve together the flour and the Backin and add these to the whisked ingredients, a tablespoon at a time.

Grease a baking sheet well and spread the mixture as thinly and evenly over it as possible (thinner than $1/4$ in. ($1/2$ cm). The mixture is enough for 2 baking sheets 12×18 in. (32×46 cm).

Oven: pre-heat for 5 minutes at very hot, bake at moderately hot.

Baking time: 15–20 minutes.

After baking for 10 minutes, cut into rectangles $1 \times 2^{1}/_{2}$ in. ($2^{1}/_{2} \times 6$ cm). Then complete baking. Remove from the baking sheet a few at a time; do not allow to cool during removal, otherwise they become brittle and break. Store in an airtight tin.

Berlin Bread

Ingredients:
2 eggs
2 tbsp. warm water
9 oz. (250 g) sugar
$2^{1}/_{2}$ oz. (70 g) "Apfelkraut" (apple preserve)
1 bottle Oetker Rum flavour
a good pinch ground allspice
a slightly heaped tbsp. ground cinnamon
$2^{1}/_{2}$ oz. (70 g) grated chocolate
9 oz. (250 g) plain flour
1 level tsp. Oetker Baking Powder Backin
$4^{1}/_{2}$ oz. (125 g) almonds or hazelnuts (left whole)
$1^{1}/_{4}$ oz. (35 g) candied lemon peel (diced)

Icing:
$3^{1}/_{2}$ oz. (100 g) icing sugar
1–2 tbsp. hot water

For the cake mixture, whisk the eggs and water until frothy, then add the sugar, a little at a time. Continue whisking until the mixture is thick and creamy. Mix and sieve together the flour and the Backin. Gradually mix in the "Apfelkraut", the flavouring and spices, the chocolate, the flour, the nuts and the candied peel. Spread the mixture about $1/4$ in. ($1/2$ cm) thick over a greased baking sheet.

Oven: pre-heat for 5 minutes at very hot, bake at moderately hot.

Baking time: 15–20 minutes.

For the icing, sieve the sugar and blend with as much of the water as will give a good coating consistency. Ice the cake while still hot and cut into slices 1×2 in. (2×5 cm).

Cinnamon Stars (uses up leftover egg whites) (Phot. page 127)

Ingredients:
3 egg whites
9 oz. (250 g) icing sugar
1 packet Oetker Vanillin Sugar
3 drops Oetker Baking Essence, bitter almond flavour
a level tsp. ground cinnamon
10–11½ oz. (275–325 g) almonds or hazelnuts (ground)
(the exact quantity of ground nuts depends upon the size of the eggs)
For rolling out:
almonds or hazelnuts (ground) or a little icing sugar

Whisk the egg whites until stiff enough to show and retain the cut of a knife. Whisk in the sieved icing sugar a tablespoon at a time. Take away 2 tbsp. to coat the stars later. Mix the vanillin sugar, the flavouring and spice and about half the nuts into the rest. Knead in so much of the ground almonds that the mixture scarcely continues to stick.
Roll out using almonds or icing sugar, instead of flour, about ¼ in. (½ cm) thick. Cut out star shapes. Line a baking sheet with greased greaseproof paper. Place the stars on this and carefully brush over with the egg white snow. If this should be too firm mix in a few drops of water.
Oven: slow.
Baking time: 20–30 minutes.
On removing from the oven the biscuits should feel soft. Store in airtight tins.

Date Macaroons (uses up leftover egg whites)

Ingredients:
3 egg whites
7 oz. (200 g) sugar
1 packet Oetker Vanillin Sugar
1 bottle Oetker rum flavour
5½ oz. (150 g) almonds (blanched and finely chopped)
5½ oz. (150 g) stoned dates (cut into tiny pieces)
3 slightly heaped tbsp. Oetker Gustin (corn starch powder)

Whisk the egg whites until stiff enough to show and retain the cut of a knife. Gradually whisk in the sugar, vanillin sugar and rum flavour. Add the almonds and dates to the egg snow and sieve the Gustin over these. Fold all gently together (do not stir or beat). Place the mixture in little heaps on a greased baking sheet, using two teaspoons.
Oven: slow.
Baking time: 50–75 minutes.

Raspeli (uses up leftover egg whites)

Ingredients:
3 egg whites
7 oz. (200 g) castor sugar
1 packet Oetker Vanillin Sugar
3 level tbsp. cocoa
5½ oz. (150 g) desiccated coconut

Whisk the egg whites until stiff enough to show and retain the cut of a knife. Whisk in the sugar and the vanillin sugar, a tablespoon at a time. Sieve the cocoa onto the egg white snow, add the coconut and fold these gently into it (do not stir or beat). Use two teaspoons to place little heaps on a greased baking sheet.
Oven: slow.
Baking time: about 25 minutes.

Fruit Bread

Ingredients:
3 eggs
4½ oz. (125 g) sugar
1 packet Oetker Vanillin Sugar
½ bottle Oetker rum flavour
a good pinch ground cinnamon
2 oz. (60 g) almonds (finely chopped)
4½ oz. (125 g) hazelnuts
   (finely chopped)
4½ oz. (125 g) figs (washed and diced)
4½ oz. (125 g) candied lemon peel
   (diced)
9 oz. (250 g) sultanas
   (washed and well drained)
4½ oz. (125 g) plain flour
5 slightly heaped tbsp. Oetker Gustin
   (corn starch powder)
1 level tsp. (7 g) Oetker Baking
   Powder Backin

Whisk the eggs until frothy, then gradually add the sugar and vanillin sugar; continue whisking until the mixture is thick and creamy (after about 15 minutes). Mix in the flavouring and spice, almonds, hazelnuts, figs, candied peel, and sultanas. Mix and sieve together the flour and Backin and add to the cake mixture. Fill into a greased loaf baking tin, lined with greased greaseproof paper.
Oven: moderately hot.
Baking time: 70–90 minutes.

Lemon Hearts (uses up leftover egg yolks) (Phot. page 127)

Ingredients:
3 egg yolks
4½ oz. (120 g) sugar
1 packet Oetker Vanillin Sugar
3 drops Oetker Baking Essence,
   lemon flavour
1 pinch Oetker Baking Powder Backin
7–9 oz. (200–250 g) almonds
   (blanched and ground)
or hazelnuts (ground)
(the exact quantity of ground nuts depends upon the size of the eggs)
For rolling out:
almonds (blanched and ground)
   or icing sugar
Lemon icing:
3½ oz. (100 g) icing sugar
1–1½ tbsp. lemon juice

For the biscuit mixture, whisk the egg yolks, sugar and the vanillin sugar until thick and creamy. Mix in the flavouring, Backin and the almonds until the mixture is too firm to mix. Knead in more of the almonds until the mixture scarcely continues to stick. Use the almonds or icing sugar to roll out instead of flour. Roll out the pastry ¼ in. (½ cm) thick and cut out heart shapes. Lay these on a baking sheet lined with well greased greaseproof paper.
Oven: pre-heat for 5 minutes at very hot,
   bake at moderately hot.
Baking time: about 10 minutes.
For the icing, blend the sieved icing sugar with as much of the lemon juice as will give a good coating consistency. Ice the biscuits while still warm.

Cedar-Bread (uses up leftover egg whites)

Ingredients:
3 egg whites
13 oz. (375 g) icing sugar
1 packet Oetker Vanillin Sugar
2 drops Oetker Baking Essence, bitter almond flavour
1 tbsp. lemon juice
grated rind of $1/2$ a lemon
about 13 oz. (375 g) almonds (blanched and ground)
For rolling out:
about $3^1/2$ oz. (100 g) almonds (blanched and ground)
Icing:
$5^1/2$ oz. (150 g) icing sugar
3–4 tbsp. lemon juice

For the biscuit mixture, whisk the egg whites until very stiff and firm enough to show and retain the cut of a knife. Whisk in the sieved icing sugar and the vanillin sugar, a tbsp. at a time. Mix in the baking essence, lemon juice and rind and a little more than half the almonds. Knead in enough of the remaining almonds to give a mixture that scarcely sticks.

Using almonds for rolling out instead of flour, roll out $1/4$ in. ($1/2$ cm) thick. Cut out halfmoon shapes and lay these on a baking sheet lined with well greased greaseproof paper.

Oven: slow.
Baking time: 30–45 minutes.
For the icing, sieve the icing sugar and blend with as much of the lemon juice as will give a good coating consistency. Ice the cooled biscuits.

Wasps' Nests (uses up leftover egg whites)

Ingredients:
3 egg whites
9 oz. (250 g) castor sugar
1 packet Oetker Vanillin Sugar
3 level tbsp. cocoa
9 oz. (250 g) almonds (blanched and finely chopped)
Smaller quantity for two people:
1 egg white
3 oz. (90 g) castor sugar
$1/2$ packet Oetker Vanillin Sugar
1 level tbsp. cocoa
3 oz. (90 g) almonds (blanched and finely chopped)

Whisk the egg whites until stiff enough to show and retain the cut of a knife. Whisk in, a spoonful at a time, the sugar and vanillin sugar. Sieve the cocoa onto the snow, add the almonds and fold gently into the egg snow. Use two teaspoons to place little heaps on a greased baking sheet.

Oven: slow.
Baking time: 25–30 minutes.

CAKE MAKING WITH YEAST

Baking with yeast is more difficult and takes longer than with Baking Powder Backin. Yeast is a living organism and needs special treatment if it is to work properly.

With Backin no special temperature is required, either for the ingredients (except that no hot ingredient may be used) or for the room in which they are being prepared. When using yeast the ingredients must be warm and the room in which they are being prepared should be at the right temperature, 99° F. (37° C.).

Just like any other living organism, yeast requires food if it is to grow and work. This food is supplied from the other ingredients in the recipe – usually sugar and flour, or starch, i. e. the carbohydrates which are to be found in the dough. When the yeast acts on these they are turned into carbon dioxide and alcohol, both of which are rising agents giving a light – textured dough. Sugar is "digested" rapidly by yeast; flour takes longer because it has to undergo certain chemical changes before it can be "digested". Fat and salt make heavy food for yeast and slow down its growth. The golden rule for cake – making with yeast is that it must never be too hot or too cold nor must the ingredients it touches be hot or cold. To make yeast work really quickly add a little sugar to the lukewarm milk. Avoid direct contact with fat or salt.

A mixture containing yeast must rise before baking. The moment the yeast comes into contact with the hot oven it "dies" and the dough will rise no more.

The dough should be left to rise in a warm place, and should never be baked directly after being prepared. It should almost double its original size.

Always bake according to the instructions in the recipe.

Yeast Cake

Cake dough:

1 oz. (30 g) yeast
1 tsp. sugar
1/4 pt. (200 ccm) and 4 tbsp. lukewarm milk
1 1/8 lb. (500 g) plain flour
5 1/2 oz. (150 g) sugar
1 packet Oetker Vanillin Sugar
4 drops Oetker Baking Essence, lemon flavour
a pinch of salt
2 eggs
4 1/2 oz. (125 g) butter, margarine or lard (melted)
1 3/4 oz. (50 g) almonds (blanched and finely chopped)
4 1/2–6 oz. (125–170 g) sultanas (washed and well drained)
1 3/4 oz. (50 g) candied lemon peel (diced)

Cream the yeast with the 1 tsp. sugar and 4 tbsp. of the milk. Sieve the flour into a large bowl, make a well in the centre and pour in the yeast. Sprinkle some of the flour over the yeast to about 1/4 in. (1/2 cm) thickness. Distribute the sugar, flavouring ingredients, eggs, and the melted fat on the flour around the well; take care that they do not come into contact with the yeast.

As soon as the flour covering the yeast shows large cracks, begin to stir all the ingredients together starting from the middle; gradually add so much of the remaining milk during mixing, until the dough is of a heavy dropping consistency. Now beat the dough with a strong wooden spoon until it shows bubbles. Fold in the almonds, sultanas and candied peel. Leave in a warm place until the dough has doubled its size. Beat again well. Dust a well-greased ring tin with bread-crumbs and fill the cake dough into it. Leave again in a warm place until the cake has doubled its size, then bake, placing as low in the oven as possible.

Oven: moderately hot.
Baking time: about 50 minutes.

Bienenstich on a Baking Sheet

Cake dough:
3/4 oz. (20 g) yeast
1 tsp. sugar
1/2 pt. (285 ccm) lukewarm milk
1 1/8 lb. (500 g) plain flour
2 1/2–3 1/2 oz. (75–100 g) sugar
3 drops Oetker Baking Essence, bitter almond flavour
a pinch of salt
1 3/4 oz. (50 g) butter, margarine or lard or 3 tbsp. oil

Topping:
3 1/2 oz. (100 g) butter or margarine
7 oz. (200 g) sugar
1 packet Oetker Vanillin Sugar
2 tbsp. milk
4 1/2–7 oz. (125–200 g) almonds (blanched and finely chopped) or hazelnuts (chopped)

Prepare the dough as for Butter or Sugar Cake – see page 174.
For the topping, melt together the fat, sugar and vanillin sugar, add the milk, mix in the nuts then set aside to cool. If the cooled topping is rather too firm stir in a little more milk; spread evenly over the cake dough.
Oven: pre-heat for 5 minutes at very hot, bake at moderately hot.
Baking time: 20–25 minutes.

Fruit Cake on a Baking Sheet

Cake dough:
3/4 oz. (20 g) yeast
1 tsp. sugar
1/2 pt. (285 ccm) lukewarm milk
1 1/8 lb. (500 g) plain flour
2 1/2 oz. (75 g) sugar
1 packet Oetker Vanillin Sugar
a pinch of salt
1 3/4 oz. (50 g) butter, margarine
or
lard (melted)
or
3 tbsp. oil

Fruit topping:
2 1/8–3 1/4 lb. (1–1 1/2 kg) apples
 or plums

For sprinkling:
a little sugar

Prepare the cake dough as for Butter or Sugar Cake – see page 174.
For the topping, peel and core the apples and slice fairly thickly, or wash and stone the plums. Arrange the fruit evenly over the cake dough, remembering that plums should lie with the cut edge upwards. Allow the cake to stand in a warm place until the dough has doubled its size, then bake.
Oven: pre-heat for 5 minutes at very hot,
bake at moderately hot.
Baking time: 20–30 minutes.
Cool the baked cake a little, then sprinkle with sugar.

Filled Ring

Cake dough:
3/4 oz. (20 g) yeast
1 tsp. sugar
1/2 pt. (285 ccm) lukewarm milk
1 1/8 lb. (500 g) plain flour
3 1/2 oz. (100 g) sugar
3 drops Oetker Baking Essence,
 lemon flavour
a pinch of salt
1 egg

For the cake dough, cream the yeast with the 1 tsp. sugar and 5 tbsp. of the milk. Sieve 2/3 of the flour into a large mixing bowl. Make a well in the centre, pour in the yeast and cover with a 1/2 in. (1/4 cm) layer of flour. Distribute the sugar, flavouring, egg and lukewarm fat on the flour around the fat, ensuring that they do not come into contact with the yeast. As soon as the flour covering the yeast shows large cracks, begin to stir all the ingredients together, starting from the middle and gradually adding the milk. Beat the dough with a strong

2¹/₅ oz. (65 g) butter, margarine or
   lard (melted)
or
4 tbsp. oil
For brushing:
1 oz. (30 g) soft butter or margarine
a little tinned milk
Filling:
2 well heaped tbsp. sugar
1 packet Oetker Vanillin Sugar
2¹/₂ oz. (70 g) currants
   (washed and well drained)
2¹/₂ oz. (70 g) sultanas
   (washed and well drained)
1–1³/₄ oz. (30–50 g) almonds
   (blanched and finely chopped)

wooden spoon until it shows bubbles, then knead in the rest of the flour. If the dough should stick add a little more flour. Leave in a warm place until it has doubled its size. Knead well, then roll out to a rectangle 20 × 22 in. (50 × 55 cm). Brush over with the fat and cut in half down the middle.
For the filling, mix together the sugar, vanillin sugar, currants, sultanas, and the almonds. Distribute the filling over the two pieces of cake dough leaving a 1 in. (2 cm) border free along the two cut edges down the middle. Roll up each piece, starting at the outside and rolling inwards. Entwine the two rolls and lay them as a ring on a greased baking sheet. Brush over with milk and make cuts ¹/₂ in. (1 cm) deep in the top surface. Allow the ring to rise in a warm place until it has doubled its size, then bake.
Oven: pre-heat for 5 minutes ar very hot,
   bake at moderately hot.
Baking time: 20–30 minutes.

Crumble Cake

Ingredients:
³/₄ oz. (20 g) yeast
1 tsp. sugar
¹/₂ pt. (285 ccm) lukewarm milk
1¹/₈ lb. (500 g) plain flour
2¹/₂–3¹/₂ oz. (75–100 g) sugar
3 drops Oetker Baking Essence,
   bitter almond flavour
a pinch of salt
1³/₄ oz. (50 g) butter, margarine or
   lard or 3 tbsp. oil
2¹/₂–3¹/₂ oz. (75–100 g) sultanas
   (washed and well drained)
Crumble topping:
10¹/₂ oz. (300 g) plain flour
5¹/₂ oz. (150 g) sugar
1 packet Oetker Vanillin Sugar
a pinch of ground cinnamon
5¹/₂ oz. (150 g) butter or margarine

Prepare the cake dough as for Butter or Sugar Cake – see page 174. Knead in the sultanas with the rest of the flour.
For the topping, sieve the flour into a mixing bowl and stir in the sugar, the vanillin sugar and the cinnamon. Cut the fat into very small pieces and rub into the dry ingredients with the fingers or two forks until a crumbly mass is formed.
Distribute the crumble topping evenly over the cake dough.
Oven: pre-heat for 5 minutes at very hot,
   bake at moderately hot.
Baking time: 15–25 minutes.

Butter or Sugar Cake on a Baking Sheet

Cake dough:
3/4 oz. (20 g) yeast
1 tsp. sugar
1/2 pt. (285 ccm) lukewarm milk
1 1/8 lb. (500 g) plain flour
2 1/2–3 1/2 oz. (75–100 g) sugar
3 drops Oetker Baking Essence, bitter almond flavour
a pinch of salt
1 3/4 oz. (50 g) butter, margarine or lard or 3 tbsp. oil

Topping:
1 3/4–4 1/2 oz. (50–125 g) butter or margarine
2 1/2 oz. (75 g) sugar
1 packet Oetker Vanillin Sugar
1 3/4 oz. (50 g) almonds (blanched and chopped) or hazelnuts (chopped)

For the cake dough, cream the yeast with 1 tsp. of the sugar and 5 tbsp. of the milk. Sieve 2/3 of the flour into a large mixing bowl, make a well in the centre and pour in the yeast; cover with 1/4 in. (1/2 cm) layer of flour. Distribute the sugar, flavouring, and melted lukewarm fat on the flour around the well; take care that they do not come into contact with the yeast. As soon as the flour covering the yeast shows large cracks, begin to stir all the ingredients together, starting from the middle, and gradually adding the rest of the milk. Beat the dough with a strong wooden spoon until it shows bubbles. Knead in the rest of the flour; if the dough should be sticky add a little more flour, but not too much, the dough should remain soft. Leave in a warm place until the dough has doubled in size. Knead thoroughly again and roll out on a greased baking sheet. Place a folded piece of greaseproof paper against the dough at the open end of the baking sheet.

For the topping, either flake the fat evenly over the cake or melt it and brush it over. Mix the sugar with the vanillin sugar and the nuts and sprinkle evenly over the cake. Leave in a warm place until the cake has doubled in size, then bake.

Oven: pre-heat for 5 minutes at very hot, bake at moderately hot.
Baking time: about 15 minutes.

Yeast Plait

Cake mixture:
3/4 oz. (20 g) yeast
1 tsp. sugar
1/5 lukewarm milk
1 1/8 lb. (500 g) plain flour
2 1/2 oz. (70 g) sugar
1 packet Oetker Vanillin Sugar
2 drops Oetker Baking Essence, lemon flavour
a little salt

Mix the yeast with the tsp. sugar in 5 tbsp. of the lukewarm milk. Sieve 2/3 of the flour into a bowl and make a well in the centre. Pour the yeast mixture into the well and sprinkle flour 1 in. (1/2 cm) thick over it. Arrange the sugar, flavourings and the melted lukewarm fat or the oil on the flour around the well (these ingredients should have no direct contact with the yeast mixture).

As soon as the flour on top of the yeast mixture shows deep cracks mix together all the ingredients, starting from the middle and adding the rest of the milk. Beat the

Continued on next page

1 egg white
2½ oz. (65 g) butter, margarine or lard (melted) or 4 tbsp. oil
2½ oz. (70 g) sultanas (washed and well drained)
1 oz. (30 g) currants (washed and well drained)

For brushing:
1 egg yolk
½ tbsp. milk

dough so long with a wooden spoon till bubbles appear, then knead in the rest of the flour together with the washed sultanas and currants. If the dough should stick add a little more flour.

Allow the dough to stand in a warm place until it is twice its size, then knead well through. From ⅔ of the dough form three rolls, 18 in. (45 cm) long; plait these together and lay on a greased baking sheet. Press a hollow down the length of the middle with a rolling pin and brush this hollow with whisked egg and milk. Divide the rest of the dough into three equal parts, forming these into rolls about, 15 in. (40 cm) long. Plait these together and lay this smaller plait on the larger one. Brush over with egg and milk. Allow to stand in a warm place until twice its size, then bake.

Oven: pre-heat for 5 minutes at very hot, bake at moderately hot.
Baking time: about 35 minutes.

ALPHABETICAL INDEX OF CONTENTS

A

Almond Cookies	61
Almond Macaroons	155
Almond Ring s. Nut or Almond Ring	79
Apple Crumble Cake	27
Apple or Cherry Roll	52
Apple or Cherry Sponge Cake	21
Apple or Cherry Tart	47
Appel or Plum Cake	78
Apple Turnovers (Cottage Cheese and Oil Pastry)	79
Apple Turnovers (Cottage Cheese Pastry)	67

B

Ballbäuschen	141
Berlin Bread	157
Berlin Pancakes	141
Bienenstich	75
Bienenstich on a Baking Sheet with Yeast	162
Black and White Cookies	65
Black Forest Cherry Cake	113
Black Forest Roll	125
Brown Christmas Biscuits	147
Butter Cream-filled Cake	108
Butter or Sugar Cake on a Baking Sheet with Yeast	167

C

Cedar-Bread	160
Cheese Biscuits	68
Cheese Biscuits, Mixed	68
Cheese Puffs	139
Cherry Roll s. Apple or Cherry Roll	52
Cherry Sponge Cake s. Apple or Cherry Sponge Cake	21
Cherry Tart s. Apple or Cherry Tart	47
Chocolate Cream-filled Sponge Cake	107
Chocolate Log (Bismarck Oak)	126
Chocolate Sponge Roll	124
Cinnamon Stars	158
Coconut Cookies	32
Coconut Corners s. Nut or Coconut Corners	58
Coconut Macaroons	155
Coffee Cakes	67
Coffee Cream Cake	114
Cottage Cheese and Oil Pastry (1)	75
Cottage Cheese and Oil Pastry (2)	76
Cottage Cheese and Oil Pastry (3)	76
Cottage Cheese Cake	49
Cottage Cheese Cake s. Fruit or Cottage Cheese Cake	51
Cottage Cheese Cream Cake	111
Cottage Cheese Flan with Cream	46
Cottage Cheese Pastry	67
Cottage Cheese White Bread	48
Cream Puffs	138
Cream Waffles (Hard Waffles)	33
Crumble Cake with Cottage Cheese Filling	30
Crumble Cake with Yeast	166
Crunchies	62
Currant Wheels	80

D

Date Macaroons	158
Domino Cubes	143
Ducat Biscuits	63

E

Eberswalder Pastries	140
Eclairs	137
Eiser Cake	33
Elise Spice Cookies	156
Empress Frederick Cake	24
Extra Fine Ring Cake	19

F

Filled Flana Biscuits 58
Filled Honey Cake 147
Filled Mokka Biscuits 50
Filled Ring with Yeast 165
Filled Shells 32
Flana Biscuits, Filled................. 58
Flana-filled Sponge.................. 93
Frankfurt Ring 19
Frisian Biscuits-Light or Dark 63
Fruit Bread 159
Fruit Cake on a Baking Sheet with
    Yeast........................... 165
Fruit Crumble Cake 48
Fruit Flan (Creamy Method) 25
Fruit Flan (Kneading Method) 44
Fruit Flan (Sponge Mixture) 118
Fruit or Cottage Cheese Cake 51
Fruit Salad Flan s. Nut Cream and
    Fruit Salad Flan 117
Fruit Tartlets 56
Fruity Filled Ring 16

G

Gooseberry Cake.................... 23
Gundula Ring 78
Gustin Cake........................ 16

H

Ham Crescents 68
Ham Rolls 81
Hazelnut Ring 57
Hazelnut Roll 130
Hedgehog Roll 77
Honey and Nut Roll 129
Honey Biscuits 144
Honey-Bread...................... 143
Honey Buttons 149
Honey Cake, Filled 147
Hunter's Buns 81

I

Iced Nut Cake 30
Iced Ring Cake 22

Iced Rum Biscuits 59
Iced Spice Nuts 152

K

Kaiser's Cake 119
King's Cake 28

L

Layer Cake 26
Lebkuchen 144
Lemon-Chocolate Cake 43
Lemon Hearts 159
Lemon Slices s. Orange or
    Lemon Slices 62
Liegnitzer Cookies 148
Linzer Cake 45

M

Mandarine Slices 88
Mannheim Biscuits 66
Marble Cake....................... 15
Margaret Biscuits 32
Mixed Cheese Biscuits 68
Mocca Biscuits, Filled............... 50
Moors' Heads 131
Mutzenmandeln.................... 142

N

Nürnberger Lebkuchen.............. 151
Nussprinten 150
Nut Cake 22
Nut Cake, Iced 30
Nut Cookies 154
Nut Cream Cake and Fruit Salad Flan.. 117
Nut Ducats........................ 61
Nut or Almond Ring 79
Nut or Coconut Corners 58
Nutty Biscuits..................... 156

O

Orange Butter Cream Cake.......... 118
Orange Cake 24
Orange or Lemon Slices 62
Orange Tart 119
Ottilia Cake 29

P

Paving Stones	148
Pineapple-Cream Cake	111
Piped Biscuits	31
Poppy Seed Cake	42
Prassel Cake	60
Prince Regent Cake	25

R

Raspeli	158
Rehrücken	28
Ring Cake, Iced	22
Ring, Filled, with Yeast	165
Rodon Cake	20
Rose Cake	76
Rum Biscuits, Iced	59
Rum Sponge Cake	87

S

Sacher Cake	115
Sand Cake	21
Sand Waffles	33
Salt-Sticks	65
Sausage Rolls	80
Savoury Snacks	81
Shortbread Biscuits	31
Snacks, Savoury	81
Spekulatius	152
Spice Cookies	157
Spice Nuts, Iced	152
Spicy Ring	27
Spitz Cakes	150
Sponge Cakes	106
Sponge Fingers	130
Sponge Mixture for Rolls and Slices	123
Sponge Slices	125
Sugar Cake on a Baking Sheet with Yeast s. Butter or Sugar Cake on a Baking Sheet with Yeast	167

St

Stollen (German Christmas Cake)	154
Strawberry Cream Cake	112
Strawberry Roll	129
Strudel Pastry	55

T

Tea Biscuits	64
Terrace Biscuits	60
Truffle Cake	112
Twists	141

V

Vanilla Crescents	153
Viennese Apple Strudel	55
Viennese Poppy Seed Strudel	56

W

Wasps' Nests	160
Wine Cream-filled Sponge Cake	107
Wine-Cream Roll	124

Y

Yeast Cake	161
Yeast Plait	167

Z

Zuger Kirsch Cake	115